MORE QUICK TEAM-BUILDING ACTIVITIES FOR BUSY MANAGERS

MORE QUICK
TEAM-BUILDING
ACTIVITIES
FOR
BUSY MANAGERS

50 New Exercises That Get Results in Just 15 Minutes

BRIAN COLE MILLER

American Management Association
New York | Atlanta | Brussels | Chicago | Mexico City | San Francisco
Shanghai | Tokyo | Toronto | Washington, D. C.

Special discounts on bulk quantities of AMACOM books are available to corporations, professional associations, and other organizations. For details, contact Special Sales Department, AMACOM, a division of American Management Association, 1601 Broadway, New York, NY 10019.
Tel.: 212-903-8316. Fax: 212-903-8083.
Web site: www. amacombooks.org

This publication is designed to provide accurate and authoritative information in regard to the subject matter covered. It is sold with the understanding that the publisher is not engaged in rendering legal, accounting, or other professional service. If legal advice or other expert assistance is required, the services of a competent professional person should be sought.

Library of Congress Cataloging-in-Publication Data

Miller, Brian Cole, 1956–
    More quick team-building activities for busy managers : 50 new exercises that get results in just 15 minutes / Brian Cole Miller.
        p.   cm.
    Includes index.
    ISBN-13: 978-0-8144-7378-8
    ISBN-10: 0-8144-7378-4
    1. Teams in the workplace—Training of.   2. Group relations training.
3. Communication in organizations—Problems, exercises, etc.   4. Interpersonal communication—Problems, exercises, etc.   5. Group games.   6. Meetings.
I. Title.
    HD66.M5437   2007
    658.4'022—dc22   2007008596

Printing number

10 9 8 7 6 5 4 3 2 1

CONTENTS

Acknowledgments **ix**
Introduction **1**

Part I. Getting Ready

CHAPTER 1. How to Run a Successful Team-Building Activity **7**

STEP 1. BEFORE: SELECT A PERTINENT ACTIVITY FOR
YOUR TEAM **7**

STEP 2. BEFORE: PREPARE FOR YOUR
TEAM-BUILDING ACTIVITY **8**

STEP 3. DURING: EXPLAIN THE ACTIVITY TO THE TEAM **10**

STEP 4. DURING: CHECK FOR UNDERSTANDING
BEFORE BEGINNING **12**

STEP 5. DURING: RUN THE ACTIVITY **13**

STEP 6. DURING: DEBRIEF THE ACTIVITY **14**

STEP 7. AFTER: REINFORCE THE LEARNING
BACK ON THE JOB **16**

CHAPTER 2. What Could Go Wrong in a Team-Building Activity **17**

Part II. The Activities

CHAPTER 3. Welcoming: Introductions and Icebreakers **31**

BET YOU DIDN'T KNOW THIS **32**

CELL PHONE RINGS **35**

HAIKU **38**

HANGMAN **40**

HEADS OR TAILS **43**

HUMAN POKER **46**

I AM . . . **50**

KIDS' STUFF **53**

PENNIES AND DICE **56**

SCRAMBLE **59**

WORD COUNT **62**

CHAPTER 4. Battling: Games That Teach Healthy Competition **65**

BALLOON BATTLE **66**

CHOPSTICKS **69**

COTTON BALLS **72**

HIGHER LOWER **75**

MARSHMALLOW DODGE BALL **78**

SNAKE EYES **81**

TABLECLOTH **85**

TALL TOWERS **88**

TEAM SCORES **91**

UNSHUFFLE **95**

CHAPTER 5. Teamwork: Challenges That Require Cooperation **99**

BUTTERMILK LINE **100**

CONNECTIONS **103**

CROSSING THE LINE **106**

DOLLAR BILL **109**

HOUSE **112**

LETTER #27 **115**

LICENSE PLATES **117**

ONE SYLLABLE   **120**

PUZZLED VISION   **123**

REACH FOR THE STARS   **126**

STICK IN THE MIDDLE   **128**

CHAPTER 6. Creativity: Challenges That Encourage
Out-of-the-Box Thinking   **131**

ABCS   **132**

FAILURE STRATEGIES   **135**

FISHBOWL   **138**

FIST   **140**

JOB TITLES   **143**

MONSTERS   **146**

NEWSPAPER COSTUMES   **148**

SECRET AGENDA   **151**

STATUE MAKER   **154**

THE SWAMP   **157**

CHAPTER 7. Support: Activities to Appreciate and
Help Each Other   **161**

ANONYMOUS FEEDBACK   **162**

GARBAGE   **166**

ONE WORD   **169**

POSITIVE ENVELOPES   **172**

SECRET COACH   **175**

TOMBSTONE   **178**

TOTEM POLES   **181**

TROPHIES   **184**

Index   **187**
About the Author   **191**

ACKNOWLEDGMENTS

This is my second collection of quick team-building activities. Many of the same professionals who gave me ideas for the first one contributed here, too. Many of the same busy managers who edited and gave me feedback on the first one also helped again. Thank you Joe Davy (yes, Davy), Dawn Snyder, Lynn Jackson, Gail Cope, Sara Bonner, Bob and Diana Miller, Caroline Cofer, Dean Miller, Chris Lowe, Adam Cope, and Suzanne Famolare.

Special thanks to Mark Hansen of sparkspace in Columbus—you really do know how to get the creative juices flowing.

A big thank you Adrienne Hickey, and everyone else at AMACOM, for believing I had another volume in me when I wasn't so sure myself.

As always, thank you Family—Gail, Lynn, Roger, Theresa, Logan, Heidee, and Benjamin—for your ongoing support and love and encouragement.

Thanks most of all to you, Tim. None of this would be possible without you, and you know it!

MORE QUICK TEAM-BUILDING ACTIVITIES FOR BUSY MANAGERS

INTRODUCTION

This book is a sequel to *Quick Team-Building Activities for Busy Managers*. Like that one, this book is written for the busy manager who wants to add an element of team-building to a meeting. There are 50 more activities here, and you can expect them to be the same type and quality as before, with one significant bonus:

New for this volume are helpful hints for virtual teams. More and more teams are dispersed geographically. Team-building becomes difficult when members are not physically together. Some teams have members who never meet each other face to face. At the end of each activity is a suggestion or two on how to adjust it for a virtual team. I've included tips for conference calls, videoconferences, Internet meetings, and more.

All activities take less than 15 minutes. Busy managers and their staffs do not have hours and hours to spend working on their team. They need activities that are quick and to the point. You can conduct each activity in this book and discuss its meaning in less than 15 minutes.

Can you really get results in 15 minutes? Yes, as long as your expectations are realistic. You will not resolve long-standing issues, major personality conflicts, or deeply embedded obstacles. What will happen is that important team issues will be highlighted so you and others can see them more clearly. Seeing them is the first step to addressing them. You will also see team members be validated and their camaraderie enhanced. In the end, you will have a stronger team.

All activities can be done with only a few common materials or even none at all. Preparing for the activities will be easy. Most require nothing at all or just a pen and paper. When other materials are needed, they are always easy to obtain if you don't already have them (a deck of cards, an old newspaper, a bag of marshmallows, etc.).

All activities have one or more specific, focused objectives. Team-building activities, such as the ones in this book, are fun. However, fun should not be the only objective. There must be a learning goal for each activity (otherwise, why bother?). Each activity is designed to bring your group together as a team in some way. You can have fun while you learn and grow together.

The outline for each activity is easy to follow. Each one is presented in the same easy-to-read, bulleted format:

This is . . . explains very briefly what the activity is.

The purpose is . . . tells what the purpose or objective of the activity is.

Use this when . . . gives you clues you should look for that will tell you if this is the right activity for your group at this time.

Materials you'll need . . . tells you everything you will need for the activity (and often it's nothing).

Here's how . . . outlines, step by step, how to conduct the activity.

For example . . . illustrates how the activity may play out, so you get a good sense of what to expect.

Ask these questions . . . lists the best questions to ask afterward. Participants need to discuss what happened in the activity and what it meant in order to gain maximum learning and growth. Skip this step and you may as well just play a parlor game with your group.

Tips for success . . . includes things that will help you run the activity most effectively.

Try these variations . . . offers variations that can be used to spice it up, slow it down, add competitiveness, or otherwise alter it for a different learning experience.

For virtual teams . . . offers tips for adjusting the activity for groups that meet electronically because they cannot be in the same physical location.

As in the first book, you will not find any of these types of activities here:

NO "fish bowl" activities in which only a few participants are actively involved while everyone else watches and critiques them.

NO role-plays in which participants are given a fictitious role to act out or perform.

NO demonstrations in which the leader makes a point by demonstrating something while everyone else merely watches and then discusses.

NO outdoor activities requiring large areas, nice weather, and physically fit participants.

NO handouts to create, copy, or distribute.

NO "touchy-feely" activities in which participants have to touch each other or share personal thoughts or feelings—activities that push the manager into the role of psychologist or therapist rather than activity leader.

The first book began with two chapters that showed you how to run any team-building activity. I have added tips for dealing with virtual teams and include the same chapters here (I want you to be successful whether you buy my other book or not).

Chapter 1 gives you start-to-finish instructions on how to run any team-building activity. The instructions are divided into the three phases of running the activities:

Before the activity, you will learn how to decide which activity is best for you and your team. Why pick just any activity when you can select one that is designed specifically for your team's needs? What should you consider when selecting an activity for virtual teams? How competitive should the activity be? Then learn how to plan and prepare for the activity (even if you have only 2 minutes in the elevator to do so!).

During the activity, you will learn how to set up the activity for success—giving clear instructions, getting your participants to want to engage, and making sure they know what to do and how to do it. For virtual teams, learn how to set up the location for participation and how to work with the technology you have. Then learn what to do while the team is involved. Finally, learn to conduct the most important element of the activity: the Debrief. This is when you help the participants connect what they did in the activity with their behavior on the job. Skip this step and you lose most of the benefit of the activity.

After the activity, you will learn how to make the things learned during the activity come alive in the workplace and make sure your team truly benefits from having done the activity in the first place.

Chapter 2 gives you tips on how to avoid what most commonly can go wrong in team-building activities. Although Murphy's Law says you'll eventually hit a bump along the way, it doesn't mean you have to fail. The format for each potential problem is the same:

What if . . . describes potential problems or concerns you may face.

What you'll see . . . indicates what you will actually see and hear that tell you a problem has come up.

The most likely causes . . . identifies what usually causes the situation. Only when you know the cause can you take meaningful action.

How to prevent it from happening . . . gives ideas on how you can avoid the problem in the first place.

What to do if it happens anyway . . . offers suggestions on how to handle a problem you tried to avoid but happened anyway.

Team-building with your staff can be fun, rewarding, and productive. Seeing those creative sparks as your staff learns something important can be very exciting. Stick with it, be patient, and you will see great results, even after just a few activities!

PART ONE
GETTING READY

CHAPTER 1

How to Run a Successful Team-Building Activity

Step 1. Before: Select a pertinent activity for your team.

Why spend the time, effort, and money on an activity if you can't identify the business reason or team benefit you expect as a result? The best team-building *activity* can become the worst team-building *experience* when there is no clear objective. If all you want is to have some fun and kill some time, play a parlor game and enjoy. If you want to improve your team's effectiveness, you need to select an activity that will give you your desired results!

Start with a clear objective in mind. What, specifically, do you want your team to learn or accomplish? Think about it. Your goal should be

- ➤ Attainable by your team.
- ➤ Relevant and applicable to where they are as a team right now.
- ➤ Something that you want to reinforce long after this activity.

Plan on this activity being one of many baby steps your team will start taking now. Remember, an effective team is built primarily on trust.

Trust, and thus team-building, can rarely be accomplished in one giant leap.

Match your goal to the activity in this book that will best help you get the results you want. If there is more than one good match, do one activity now and another one at a later date.

Consider technological capabilities. For teams that are geographically dispersed (virtual teams), consider whether the technology you use includes video, audio, and/or text capacity. Select activities that are compatible with your technology so that it doesn't get in the way of the team-building efforts.

A NOTE ON COMPETITION: Competition can be a good thing. It can excite, energize, and challenge people to participate better. Do not assume that competition naturally brings out the best in everyone, though. Competition can also be a bad thing. It can deflate, discourage, and create unnecessary, lingering conflict. As the final judge in competitive activities, you risk becoming "the bad guy" as well. So only you can say how competitive you want your team-building activity to be. The most important thing is to be deliberate in your decision, so you can justify it with a clear objective, if necessary. Consider:

- ➤ The current level of competition within the team.
- ➤ The emotional health of the participants in dealing with defeat.
- ➤ How intimidating or intimidated the participants are.
- ➤ Your ability to diffuse real conflict among the team.
- ➤ How easy it will be for participants to cheat if they are geographically dispersed and how much the participants trust each other to play fairly.

Step 2. Before: Prepare for your team-building activity.

You want to make sure you are ready for everyone to have a great learning experience. Fifteen minutes of planning and preparation ahead of time may not guarantee success, but it will certainly help you prevent disaster. Your activity will be most effective if you go into it feeling competent and confident.

Read through the entire activity several times. Make sure you are clear on what is to happen, when, why, and how. Visualize that activity happening successfully.

Obtain all necessary materials. Check the materials to make sure they will work well for the activity. For example, see that the dates on the pennies are legible, test the markers for any that have dried out, make sure there are no cards missing from the deck, and so forth. Assume nothing! Always have a few extras on hand, just in case. If you have to ship materials to other locations for virtual team-building, do so in plenty of time. Confirm their arrival before the meeting.

Practice what you are going to say when you start the activity with your team. The best way to do this is to explain the activity to friends or colleagues. If they don't understand you, figure out a way to explain things more clearly until they do. If you plan to conduct the activity with a virtual team, it's best to do a trial run with a partner in another location and with the same technology that will be used. Work out the kinks now!

If the activity requires you to have a role (card dealer, judge, moderator, etc.), practice your comments or actions. This will help you feel less nervous during the activity. It will also free your mind to focus on more important things (the participants' reactions, the participants' learning, your own observations, etc.) during the activity.

Set up the room. Make sure the tables, chairs, flip charts, and other items are placed so that they contribute to the activity's success. A classroom style row of chairs is usually the least conducive to team-building activities. Better choices include a large circle, a "U" shape, or small table groups (several individuals gathered around each table). Any specific setup information required for an activity is noted within that activity. For virtual teams, coordinate the setup with the other locations beforehand.

If the activity's rules or steps are lengthy, write them ahead of time, and post them on the wall so that everyone can see them throughout the activity. Send the rules or steps ahead of time to the other locations when you are working with virtual teams.

Anticipate potential problems. Visualize the activity with *your* team, in *your* location(s). Ask yourself what could go wrong. Take action to prevent those problems from occurring, and plan the corrective actions you can take if they do occur. The most common problems, and how to avoid or deal with them, are discussed in the next chapter.

Plan on taking more time when working with virtual teams. Any type of meeting done via conference calling, video conferencing, or on the Internet will require more time than if it is conducted in person. It takes longer for people to converse with each other by these means. Team-building is no exception. Expect each activity presented here to take 5–10 minutes longer when done electronically.

Step 3. During: Explain the activity to the team.

A 1-minute introduction can make all the difference in setting your team up for success! People engage better when they know *why* they are doing something. They also participate better when they understand all the rules up front and when they are clear on exactly what is expected of them.

Set the mood. Welcome the team with enthusiasm and optimism. Team-building is fun! Convey this right away. You don't have to be a cheerleader; even a smile or a warm comment will let your team know they are in for a great time.

Explain the activity. Give a very brief overview of what you have planned so that the participants can start getting interested and excited.

Explain why you are doing this particular activity. Share what you hope to accomplish in the next 15 minutes. The more the participants see purpose to the activity (it's not just for fun or to kill time), the more likely they will be engaged and learn what you want them to learn. For a few of the activities in this book, you will ruin their impact by sharing the objective up front. In these cases, explain that there is an objective that will become clear in a few minutes. Make sure that the objective is called out during the Debrief (the discussion that is held immediately after the activity).

Explain the activity's rules or steps. Don't be afraid to read from this book, use notes, or even have notes posted on the wall (send them ahead of time to remote locations for virtual teams). Speak slowly, and pause after each step. Remember, the team hasn't had time to read and reread the activity like you have. It's usually easier to explain the activity all at once, before responding to any questions from the team.

Have the team move through each of the activity's steps as you explain it. For example, if the first step of an activity is to divide the group into smaller teams, have them actually do this before you tell them the next step. Go slower for virtual teams; they don't have the benefit of being in the same room as you.

A NOTE ON TEAM SIZE: Most activities will not be ruined if smaller groups are not exactly the same size. If the correct size is critical, the odd participant or two could be assigned the role of "Observer." The Observer role is to quietly watch the others participate. During the Debrief, the Observers share their unique observations. Usually for virtual teams, the obvious split is done geographically. Just be aware that while this may pull the participants in each location together, it may also foster their competitiveness with other locations.

NOTES ON PAIRING UP: When an activity requires the participants to pair up, use your own participation to even things out. Participate if the number is odd; observe if it is even. In addition, when virtual teams are able to communicate directly with each other via instant messaging, e-mail, or telephone, it's a good idea to pair them up with participants in other locations.

Distribute the materials after you've fully explained the activity. Otherwise, you risk people getting distracted by them and missing key points. Distribute the materials before the explanation only if you have found that the materials help people understand things better.

Step 4. During: Check for understanding before beginning.

People often hesitate to ask for help when they are confused. You can clarify misunderstandings with patience and some simple review questions. You can keep competition from getting out of hand by laying down a few ground rules, but they must be agreed upon up front.

Make sure your team understands the activity. Asking, *"Do you understand?"* is the least effective way to check this (who wants to answer *"No"* in front of the group?). *"Do you have any questions?"* is a little better. *"What questions do you have?"* is even better still.

However, the best way to check their understanding is to ask questions that force the team to review the steps or rules of the activity. For example, *"How many minutes do you have to complete this?"* or *"What happens if one of your balloons pops?"*

For virtual teams, check in with each location specifically. Participants who are in the same room as you are more likely to understand you than are those in other locations. So spread your questions to every location. Make sure everyone everywhere is on the same page before you begin. If you don't, a disaster is likely.

When the activity will result in one or more winners, make sure everyone is clear on what criteria will be used to determine who wins. Then, ask a review question such as *"How exactly does someone win?"* If ties need to be broken, explain how this will be done.

Declare up front that you are the final judge on all disagreements about who wins. You don't want participants to argue about who won, thereby losing focus on the real purpose of the activity.

When you are confident everyone understands the activity and is ready to go, ask one last time, *"What remaining questions do you have before we start?"*

Step 5. During: Run the activity.

Letting the team go through the activity, and possibly even fail, may be difficult for you. Remember, the activity is a low-risk alternative to letting the participants learn from failures on the job! People learn and retain better when they experience lessons rather than just hear about them. Sit back, observe, and let your team experience.

Once the participants begin the activity, see that they are following the steps or rules. You want them to at least get started down a path to success. Hold off on correcting them for just a moment, though. They may check themselves. If not, gently bring them back to task. This will be more difficult at remote locations for virtual teams. Depending on the activity, you may want to assign someone at each location to help you facilitate the activity. If not, you may establish a "check-in" time part way through the activity. All teams stop briefly to report their progress. This will allow you to gauge if they are on track or not.

Encourage and support them all. Especially thank anyone who goes first in an activity. Being first is a scary situation for many. It takes courage to go first and risk embarrassment or failure.

Make yourself available to clarify steps or to redirect the team. If appropriate, wander around quietly and watch for opportunities to help everyone be successful. Be careful not to do their task for them, though. When working with virtual teams, don't be afraid to check in often.

Throughout the activity, watch and listen for things you will want to bring up during the Debrief. It is OK to jot down a note or two to remember. If you have helpers at other locations with a virtual team, ask them to do this as well.

If the activity is timed, watch the clock and give a "time check" occasionally. For example, *"Time check: you have 2 minutes left."*

Don't stop the activity unless it really runs amuck. Otherwise, let it run its course. There will be plenty of opportunity during the Debrief to comment on lessons learned.

Step 6. During: Debrief the activity.

The Debrief is the most critical part of the team-building activity. It is the time when effective questions will guide the participants to link what they experienced in the activity with their behavior on the job. If this step is skipped or glossed over, most of the impact of the activity will be lost in a matter of days. If you conduct the Debrief well, the lessons learned during the activity will impact the team indefinitely.

Ask the questions outlined in this book immediately. For most questions, there is no right or wrong answer. Let all answers be OK. Try not to evaluate or critique any answer; just nod and accept each one as you hear it. The questions for each activity should lead the participants to the conclusion you want them to reach without you having to spell it out for them.

It is fine to read the questions from this book or to use notes. Simply stop talking, silently read the question, look back at the team, and then ask the question. The few seconds of silence while you read are less noticeable and less offensive to the group than if you read the question aloud while looking at it. Also, making eye contact while you ask the question is more likely to result in a response than if you do it the other way.

Another way to ask the questions is to write them on index cards beforehand. Pass the index cards out, and ask the participants to take turns reading the questions and soliciting responses. For virtual teams, e-mail the questions.

Try not to call on anyone by name unless you have to. Be comfortable with the silence. Once you have asked a question, stop talking and slowly count to 10 in your head. The silence may feel like an eternity to you, but it feels just as long to the group. Eventually someone will answer! Remember, they have never heard the question before, so it may take a few seconds to formulate a response. Be patient.

For virtual teams, you may have to direct your questions to individuals or at least to specific locations. It will be natural for those in the room with you to engage more readily than those at other locations. Encourage those at other locations to participate. You may want to specifically ask them to respond before you ask anyone at your location. Don't require a response to each and every question from each and every location, though. If you do, participants will only give minimal responses just to satisfy the requirement.

The silences between responses will be longer with virtual teams. Participants will pause more before speaking, making sure they don't interrupt someone else. Be patient and plan on it taking a bit longer than if everyone was in the same room together.

Watch for heads nodding, smiles, and other indications that participants agree with what is being said by others. Not everyone has to respond to every question for the entire group to learn. For virtual teams, just check in with them. *"I see a lot of heads nodding here. What about there in Maine? Seattle? San Juan?"* If you see reactions that suggest disagreement, ask, *"Does anyone disagree? What about an opposing view? Are you guys at Belfield Drive in agreement, too?"* Call on the one disagreeing only as a last resort.

Repeat or quickly summarize each response offered. This is especially critical when working with virtual teams unless the activity is done in text only.

If anyone gives an off-the-wall response or one that is just plain wrong, ask the group how they feel about it rather than correcting someone. This technique will keep it "safe" for all participants to continue answering questions without fear of a reprimand from you.

Even if the activity did not go quite as well as planned, most participants probably learned something. No matter what happened, you can always ask if the group has ever seen anything like this happen back on the job. Ask what can be learned from this experience. The answers may include what can be improved for future team-building activities!

Step 7. After: Reinforce the learning back on the job.

With your help, the activity can continue teaching the participants long after it is over. Reminding participants of the activity and keeping the lessons learned alive will extend its impact. Keep your team focused on behaviors that support the kind of team you are trying to build.

Display anything the team created for the activity back in the workplace. Each time they see that sculpture, flip chart, or cardboard structure, they will be reminded of what they did, how it made them feel, and what it taught them. For virtual teams, send the results around to each other.

If any new terms or special words came up during the activity, use them frequently. Like the visual items, these words will prompt a memory of what happened and what they learned.

Refer to the activity and to the lessons learned often when you are coaching, giving feedback, or conducting staff meetings. Look for examples of people exhibiting good team behavior related to the activity, and call it out for them and others to see.

If the activity was a huge success, you may want to repeat it soon.

Plan follow-up activities that will reinforce, emphasize, and build upon what was learned this time.

Watch for examples of how the participants used what they learned in the activity and got better results. If you can quantify how their actions are benefiting the organization, call it out for them and others as evidence of success.

Ask participants in your next staff meeting to share what impact the activity has had on them. For remote locations, use e-mail, electronic bulletin boards, and so forth to keep the learning alive.

CHAPTER 2

What Could Go Wrong in a Team-Building Activity

The team-building activities in this book are easy to conduct in most situations. They have been used successfully with hundreds of other groups just like yours. Follow the instructions carefully, and you will be successful, too!

If you have never run such activities before, it is natural to be concerned about what could go wrong. Below are the most common fears and problems managers face running an activity. Channel the energy your concerns generate into positive actions to avoid problems and/or to effectively deal with them if they do happen!

What if . . .   One or more people don't want to participate?

What you'll   ➤ Eye rolling.
see . . .   ➤ Lack of eye contact with you or other negative
                      body language.
              ➤ With virtual teams, silence from other locations.
              ➤ Expressions of isolation or feeling less important
                  by virtual team members.
              ➤ Negative comments about the activity or team-
                  building in general.

> Direct comments that they do not want to participate.

> Direct refusal to participate.

> Participants dragging their feet to get started.

> Suggestions for an alternate activity ("*Why don't we just . . .*").

The most likely causes . . .

> Past unpleasant or unproductive team-building experiences.

> Lack of understanding the purpose or value of the activity.

> Shyness or fear of being embarrassed.

> The activity doesn't sound fun or worthwhile.

How to prevent this from happening . . .

> Be clear on the purpose of the activity when you introduce it to the group.

> Be sure the purpose of the activity is one that is needed or valued by the group.

> Reassure the group that everyone will do it (and no one will be singled out to be embarrassed).

> Reassure participants in other locations of their importance. Go out of your way to include them if the activity is being done with them not in the same room.

> If it's an activity that allows this, have the less shy people go first.

> If you expect resistance from a particular individual, privately approach him or her beforehand to gain a commitment to participate.

What to do if it happens anyway . . .

> Unless it's critical, don't make a big deal of it; perhaps after witnessing one or two effective team-building activities, these people will become more willing to participate next time.

> Remind them that in order for it to be team-building, everyone must participate; otherwise,

the rest of the group won't benefit from the exercise.

➤ Let the group know someone doesn't want to participate, and allow them to handle it. (Beware, the members may apply more pressure than you would, or they may allow the person to not participate at all.)

➤ Find a way for the person to still be involved—perhaps as Scorekeeper, or Timekeeper, or Observer (with the expectation that he or she will offer observations after the activity).

What if . . .	They don't understand the directions I am giving?
What you'll see . . .	➤ Confused looks. ➤ Participants asking each other what to do. ➤ Silence from other locations (with virtual teams). ➤ Participants not doing what is expected. ➤ Nothing happening when the activity begins. ➤ Lots of questions for clarification.
The most likely causes . . .	➤ Directions were given out of order. ➤ Directions were poorly explained. ➤ Side bar conversations distracted attention. ➤ Directions were given too fast. ➤ Directions were too lengthy and not posted. ➤ Technological difficulties occurred (with virtual teams).
How to prevent this from happening . . .	➤ Read and reread the directions to make sure *you* understand them well. ➤ Post the directions or rules (with virtual teams, send ahead to other locations). ➤ Practice explaining the activity to others until they readily understand. Use their questions to help you adjust the way you explain it next time.

➤ Pause after each direction to let it sink in.
➤ Check and double-check any technological equipment that will be used ahead of time.
➤ Speak slowly as you explain the activity.
➤ Repeat what seems like the obvious when you give directions (e.g., *"First I want you to pair up. That means we need everyone in a group of two—find one partner to be with right now."*).

What to do if it happens anyway . . .
➤ Start over. Repeat all the directions, so the difficult ones are put into context. This time, slow down even more.
➤ Ask someone who did understand to help you explain.
➤ Do not get frustrated (either with yourself or with the team). Stay calm and focused. Be patient with yourself and with them until you are successful.
➤ Read the directions from the book. If you got it from the book, they will also.
➤ If a technology fails, use the backup.
➤ If applicable, demonstrate the activity.

What if . . .
Materials break or don't work, or we don't have enough?

What you'll see . . .
➤ Not enough materials to go around.
➤ Materials breaking or not functioning as planned.

The most likely causes . . .
➤ Not planning ahead.
➤ Underestimating the number of materials needed.
➤ Using the wrong materials.

How to prevent this from happening . . .
➤ Bring more than enough materials for all possible participants; err with too many rather than too few.
➤ Practice or test the activity with the exact materials or equipment that will be used (within the same

timeframe) to make sure they will perform the way you expect.

➤ For virtual teams, send the materials in plenty of time. Then confirm their arrival.

What to do if it happens anyway . . .
➤ Use spare materials (if you have extras).
➤ Improvise with other materials, if possible.
➤ Adjust the rules of the activity, if possible.
➤ Reschedule the activity.

What if . . .
➤ Someone gets overly competitive?

What you'll see . . .
➤ One person taking the activity too seriously.
➤ Someone bending the rules, or even cheating.
➤ Extreme efforts to win or to do better than others.
➤ Participants overly discussing the activity afterward, with a focus on strategies and missed opportunities rather than on learning points.

The most likely causes . . .
➤ A naturally competitive environment in the workplace (e.g., a sales force).
➤ Naturally competitive people.
➤ Conflict in the group.
➤ Too much focus on the activity rather than on learning.

How to prevent this from happening . . .
➤ Make sure the rules for tiebreakers are very clear up front.
➤ Focus the group's attention on the activity's purpose and learning goals when you introduce it.
➤ For a naturally competitive group, select activities that encourage teamwork or that have a lesser element of competition built into them.
➤ Offer a very minimal prize for the winner during the introduction that will not be a lingering reminder (e.g., an exactly 3-second round of applause rather than a candy bar).

What to do if it happens anyway . . .	➤ Focus the Debrief on what happened, why it happened, group dynamics, and so forth, rather than on who won or who did better than who (you may even have to declare *"Let's take the focus off the activity itself and discuss what we learned from the activity."*).
	➤ Discuss the competitiveness that came out, why it came out, and how helpful or destructive it was. Link these things back to the workplace.
	➤ If you must, stop the activity in the middle to remind the group of the activity's purpose and learning goals.
What if . . .	Participants don't join the Debrief discussion?
What you'll see . . .	➤ Lack of eye contact with you, especially right after you ask a question.
	➤ Silence from one or more locations (with virtual teams)
	➤ Minimal or one-word responses to your questions.
	➤ Shoulder shrugging.
	➤ Silence.
The most likely causes . . .	➤ They didn't understand your question.
	➤ You haven't given them enough time to formulate an answer.
	➤ They fear embarrassment of a "wrong" answer in front of you or their peers.
	➤ They are angry about something (which may be unrelated to the activity).
How to prevent this from happening . . .	➤ Ask questions slowly.
	➤ Don't be afraid to read the questions from the book.
	➤ Pause (silently count to 10) after each question. This pause may feel like an eternity to you, but it will give participants the time they need to consider an appropriate response.

> Unless they are too far off, accept and appreciate all responses. This is an opportunity to appreciate the diverse thinking styles of your team!

> For virtual teams, encourage those in the same room as you to remain quiet at first so that people in other locations have a chance to speak up.

What to do if it happens anyway . . .

> Reword or restate questions only if the group tells you that they didn't understand the question; otherwise, let them think.

> As a last resort, call on participants by name to respond.

> Explain that the activity is only as valuable as their ability to transfer what they learned from it back to the workplace. They can start doing this by discussing the questions.

> After asking a question, offer your own observation. Then ask what others saw that was similar to or different from what you just shared.

> When you get responses, emphatically thank the first few participants for contributing.

> For virtual teams, start directing questions to specific locations.

What if . . .   Someone dominates the Debrief?

What you'll see . . .

> One person answering most of the questions.
> One person talking excessively.
> Most participants remaining silent.

The most likely causes . . .

> The person wanted to help you (and the team) by offering the answers.
> The person wanted to show that he or she had the correct answers.
> Other participants didn't volunteer answers.

- Other participants were afraid to differ with the dominant person.
- The person was impatient waiting for others to contribute.
- The person didn't feel like he or she was being heard or taken seriously.
- The person may dominate the group in day-to-day work, and this was just an extension of the group norm.

How to prevent this from happening . . .

- After anyone answers a question, ask, *"What do the rest of you think?"* or *"What else?"* as you make eye contact with other participants. This will give the signal that you are looking for more discussion than just one answer per question.
- Repeat or quickly summarize each comment and then say, *"Great, who else has an observation?"*
- Be comfortable yourself waiting for others to respond (a few seconds of silence may encourage others to speak).
- If you expect a particular person to dominate the discussion, consider talking to that person before the activity and ask him or her to hold back, or encourage others to contribute.
- If the person tends to dominate day to day, begin to address this behavior outside the confines of this activity.
- For virtual teams, this most often happens with someone in the same room as you. Encourage people in the other locations to participate by not allowing your room participants to respond until someone from another location does so first.

What to do if it happens anyway . . .

- When asking questions, avoid making eye contact with the dominant one.
- Begin a few questions with, *"OK, for the rest of you, my next question is. . . ."*

> Call on a few participants for their thoughts.
> In an extreme case, ask the person to hold off speaking until others have had a chance to respond.
> Ask, *"Who has a different perspective he or she would like to share with us?"*

What if . . .   The Debrief gets out of hand?

What you'll see . . .
> A gripe session.
> Arguing or fighting.
> Discussion moving off the topic.
> Side bar discussions.
> With virtual teams, people at one location can go off on their own tangent or "take on" the other teams.

The most likely causes . . .
> Poor questions asked during the Debrief.
> Unresolved issues in the team.
> Lost control.

How to prevent this from happening . . .
> Unless you are a skilled facilitator, don't veer too far from the questions in this book.
> Do not host activities as a means to resolve deep issues in the team.
> Ask one or more team members beforehand what kind of reaction they believe the activity will spark in the team.
> Avoid questions that will put anyone on the spot.
> Avoid questions that pit anyone against anyone else.

What to do if it happens anyway . . .
> Step in and stop the discussion(s) before more damage is done; ask, *"How does your discussion apply to what we learned from the activity?"*
> Don't try to assign blame or find the cause.

> Refocus the Debrief with specific, targeted questions (use the questions in this book).

> With virtual teams, it may be appropriate to acknowledge that participants in a specific location have an issue that needs to be resolved. Commit to addressing it later, and move on.

> In a severe case, terminate the activity and Debrief altogether. This may be an ideal time to try to identify the issues at play and to figure out what activities to use next.

What if . . . They don't get what I wanted them to get out of the activity?

What you'll see . . .
> Incorrect answers are given during the Debrief.
> No connection is made between the activity and the workplace.
> Key participant behaviors or actions during the activity go unnoticed.

The most likely causes . . .
> The purpose of the activity was not explained well up front.
> The activity was not the best one to bring out the learning you wanted.
> The Debrief questions were not handled well.

How to prevent this from happening . . .
> Be sure to explain the purpose of the activity to the team. Get participants to buy into the need to engage and learn.
> Be sure you have a clear learning objective and that the activity you choose will help your team achieve it.
> Let the participants answer the Debrief questions rather than you spoon-feed the correct responses to them.

- When you get minimal responses to Debrief questions, ask for clarification or elaboration.
- Avoid helping the participants get through the activity. The more you help, the less they experience, and thus the less they learn and grow.

What to do if it happens anyway . . .
- Disclose to the group what lesson you had hoped to teach, and discuss where that lesson was found in the activity.
- Let it go; accept what they did learn and build upon that.
- If time permits, redo the activity with a renewed focus on the desired objective.

A FINAL NOTE: Remember, your participants want their activity to be successful just as much as you do!

PART TWO

THE ACTIVITIES

CHAPTER 3

Welcoming: Introductions and Icebreakers

BET YOU DIDN'T KNOW THIS

This is . . .	An icebreaker activity in which participants share little-known facts about themselves.
The purpose is . . .	For participants to learn something interesting about each other. This information may prompt some small talk later.
Use this when . . .	➤ Individuals already know each other at least a little bit.
	➤ A new team is forming, especially with participants who already know each other.
	➤ People seem bored with each other and need a boost of energy.
Materials you'll need . . .	➤ One index card for each participant.
	➤ A straight pin (or tape) for each participant.
	➤ A pen or pencil for each participant.
Here's how . . .	1. Divide the group into two teams.
	2. Give everyone an index card.
	3. Have all participants write one little-known fact about themselves on their card.
	4. Collect all the cards from Team 1 and Team 2. Place the stack of Team 2's cards aside for now.

5. Randomly distribute Team 1's cards to Team 2, keeping them face down (so participants can't read them).
6. Have the Team 2 participants pin the card they have on their back, written side showing (so that everyone can read the card except the one wearing it).
7. All the participants mingle. Each Team 1 member finds his or her card on the back of a Team 2 member and pairs up with that person.
8. When paired up, the Team 2 member asks the Team 1 member yes/no questions to determine (guess) what is written on the card.
9. Repeat the process for Team 2's cards.

Ask these questions . . .

➤ How much did you learn about each other? *(I had no idea that she . . . ; I don't want to mess with this guy; Looks are deceiving!)*

➤ How difficult (or easy) was it to guess what was on your card? *(Harder than I thought, because I kept wanting to ask more open questions; Easy once I figured out it was a sport she liked.)*

➤ What questions helped you the most? *(Questions that were broader; Questions that didn't assume too much to begin with; Just asking lots of questions fast.)*

➤ Why do you think it's important to get to know each other here at work beyond just knowing the tasks that each other performs? *(Because we work with the whole person, not just a part of that person; So we can enjoy our time together more; It allows us to appreciate each other better.)*

➤ How can we get to know each other back on the job?

Tips for success . . .

➤ After each round, give the group a little time for discussion. Many people will have read the cards that others wrote and be curious who wrote this one or that one. Undoubtedly, there will be a few stories that simply *must* be told!

➤ Make sure no one looks at or reads the card that goes on his or her back.

Try these variations . . .

➤ Have participants write two statements on their card, one true and one false. Follow the same procedure, but, after the wearer has guessed both statements, he or she then must guess which one is true and which one is not.

➤ At Step 2, rather than a little-known fact, have participants write a provocative question. At Step 7, Team 1 participants do not pair up with whoever is wearing their card. Instead, everyone mingles freely. As participants read the questions on others' backs, they merely respond to the question (without telling what the question was). Team 2 participants are challenged with guessing what the question on their back is.

➤ At Step 2, have the participants write a fact that is well known about themselves. At Step 7, Team 2 participants mingle with Team 1 participants and ask them yes/no questions about the fact on their back. The challenge is to guess what is written and who wrote it.

For virtual teams . . .

This activity works well for groups that are able to communicate with each other via instant messaging, e-mail, or telephone.

1. Pair everyone up.
2. Person A keeps his or her information secret while Person B asks the yes/no questions.
3. Each of the variations listed can work for a virtual team.

CELL PHONE RINGS

This is . . . A fun introduction or icebreaker activity in which participants introduce themselves by playing their cell phone ring.

The purpose is . . . For participants to learn a little bit about each other that is not work related.

Use this when . . .
➤ Participants don't know each other well.
➤ You want the participants to warm up, begin talking to each other and connecting without getting too personal or intrusive.
➤ You don't have prep time and/or materials for anything more elaborate.

Materials you'll need . . .
➤ Each participant needs a cell phone.

Here's how . . .
1. Have each participant introduce himself or herself with relevant information (name, position, location, etc.).
2. The participant then plays his or her cell phone ring tone and explains why he or she chose that particular tone.

For example . . . "My name is Lynn. This is my cell phone ring. I chose this one because I'm often outside watching my son's baseball games. If my phone rings in my purse, I need it to be loud and obnoxious so that I'm sure to hear it!"

Ask these questions . . .

- ➤ Why did you choose that ring tone? *(I wanted something that reminded me of the telephone ring I heard when I was a kid; It just came with the phone, and I never changed it; My son likes to change it on me periodically.)*
- ➤ Do you have separate ring tones for special individuals or numbers? *(No, I hardly know how to change this one; Yes, so I can know ahead of time if I want to answer or not; No, that would take too long to set up.)*
- ➤ When do you turn your phone to vibrate? Off altogether? *(As a single mother, I never turn it off completely; I turn it off in meetings; I only use it to make emergency calls, so I rarely ever turn it on.)*
- ➤ How can we get to know more about each other back on the job?

Tips for success . . .

- ➤ This may be a great way to introduce the idea of turning off the cell phones during the meeting. After the tone is played, the phone goes off (or to vibrate)!
- ➤ Be prepared to call others' numbers to make the phone ring—not everyone will know how to demonstrate the ring tone.
- ➤ This can be a fun way to introduce or reinforce policies about cell phone usage in the workplace.

Try these variations . . .

- ➤ Rather than sharing cell phone tones, pass around your cell and show everyone your favorite picture that is saved on it.
- ➤ Make a list of everyone's cell number. Put all the cell phones in the center of a circle. Use your

phone to call any number on the list. Upon hearing the tone, the owner retrieves his or her phone and then explains the reason for that tone. (This is especially fun if more than one person has the same tone!) Then he or she calls another number on the list, and the game continues.

For virtual teams . . . This activity works well when the technology used includes audio capability.

1. Follow the steps above.
2. A variation: Gather everyone's cell number. Randomly call the numbers. The owners of the numbers tell the group about their ring tone.
3. A variation: Participants take a picture of themselves with their cell phone and send it to each other. Participants then comment on what they are wearing and why, or on what is in the background, or about what the look on their face really means!

HAIKU

This is . . .	An introduction or icebreaker activity in which participants create a haiku poem to introduce or describe themselves.
The purpose is . . .	For participants to get to know each other a little better while expressing themselves more creatively than most icebreakers allow.
Use this when . . .	➤ The group appreciates a creative challenge. ➤ The group is being too linear and needs to think more freely and creatively. ➤ You don't have prep time and/or materials for anything more elaborate.
Materials you'll need . . .	➤ No materials are necessary for this activity.
Here's how . . .	1. Give participants 4–8 minutes to create a haiku that introduces or describes themselves. 2. Have a poetry reading. Each participant reads his or her haiku.
For example . . .	Football can be dull Until the marching band plays. Then Heidee's happy. Benjamin's my name. Video games and lacrosse, That's what I live for. Be on the lookout . . . Logan's gonna be a star. Just you watch and see.

Ask these questions . . .	➤ How difficult (or easy) was it for you to limit what you share about yourself to so few words? *(Easy because it was so short; It was hard to think of something that people don't already know about me.)*
	➤ How did you narrow down your scope to the one thing that you included? What did you not include but would have liked to? *(It all depended on what I could fit in five syllables; I picked what was most important to me—my family; I couldn't decide what to talk about so I made two haiku.)*
	➤ How did the structure of the haiku affect what you shared? *(It was so limiting; It made me boil it down to the essence; It helped me keep from rambling.)*
	➤ How can we apply this creativity that we learned today back on the job?
Tips for success . . .	➤ Haiku poems have three lines. The first and last lines have exactly five syllables each. The middle line has exactly seven syllables. The poems rarely, if ever, rhyme.
	➤ This activity can work in any language, not just English (or Japanese, in which it originated).
	➤ Post the poems where others can see and appreciate them.
Try these variations . . .	➤ Award prizes for most clever, most revealing, most beautiful, most funny, and so forth. (Don't let participants vote for their own haiku.)
	➤ Use poetry formats other than haiku—Roses are red; There once was a man from Nantucket; Hickory Dickory Dock; Jack and Jill; Little Miss Muffet; and so forth.
	➤ Have each participant write his or her haiku on a flip chart page. Then have others draw pictures or designs to enhance the haiku.
For virtual teams . . .	This activity works well regardless of the technology used. If audio is not available, participants can type in their haiku.

HANGMAN

This is . . . An introduction or icebreaker activity in which participants play a variation of the traditional hangman game—others will draw the body parts on the hangman victim.

The purpose is . . . For participants to learn new, interesting, and obscure facts about each other while warming up for a meeting or training.

Use this when . . .
- ➤ Participants don't know each other very well.
- ➤ The group needs to warm up for a meeting.
- ➤ The group needs an activity to get moving and energized.

Materials you'll need . . .
- ➤ One piece of paper for each participant.
- ➤ One colored marker for each participant.

Here's how . . .
1. Give each participant a piece of paper and a marker.
2. Have everyone draw a large gallows.
3. Then, encourage participants to mingle.
4. Have another participant draw the head for your hangman and share one story about himself or herself that has to do with his or her head.
5. Have a different participant draw the torso for your hangman and share one story about his or her own body.

6. Have a third person draw one leg or one arm for your hangman and share one story about his or her own arm or leg.

7. Continue collecting the other arms and legs until your hangman is complete.

For example . . .
"Here is your arm. When I was a little girl, my brother and I were coming in the garage door and I put my hand on the doorjamb. The wind took the door and slammed it shut and really wrecked up my thumb. See? I still have scars from it."

"OK, here's your leg. I recently hired a personal trainer to help me get stronger. He kept commenting on how strong my legs were getting. A few weeks ago I squatted 405 pounds, which is quite a lot of weight for a man my age!"

Ask these questions . . .
➤ How difficult (or easy) was it to share stories about yourself? *(Pretty easy once I remembered the story about my head; Hard because everyone needed a story about a leg and I couldn't think of one to help them.)*
➤ Did you share the same story about a specific body part with everyone, or did you change stories each time? Why? *(The same one, it just made it easier; The same one because it's so funny; I tried to think of a different one so I could help them with whatever body part they needed.)*
➤ Why is important to get to know each other outside our strict work roles?

Tips for success . . .
➤ If there are enough participants, make the rule that you can get only one body part from each person (so that someone doesn't draw half of the hangman and monopolize the time with his or her stories!).

➤ Offer an example or two of the type of stories you're looking for (use real-life stories of your own).

➤ There should be some order to the drawing. For example, the head must be first, followed by the torso. Then, the arms and legs can be drawn in any order.

Try these variations . . .

➤ Instead of drawing a hangman, draw a house, an office, a vacation destination, or your organization's product or service. The stories then deal with the part of the house, destination, and so forth.

➤ Besides the basics (head, torso, legs, arms), include more details to the hangman (hands, feet, facial features, etc.).

➤ Make it more difficult by not allowing anyone to repeat a story.

➤ For a group that is well acquainted, require that the stories be about another group member's body part rather than their own.

For virtual teams . . .

This activity works well for groups that are able to communicate with each other via instant messaging, e-mail, or telephone.

1. Participants mingle in the main chat room, on the main conference call, or wherever the whole group is congregating. Once participants pair up, they can use whatever technology is available to have the one-on-one conversation.

2. Then follow Steps 4–7 except that participants draw their own hangman as they listen to the stories from their partner.

3. Each of the variations listed can work for a virtual team.

HEADS OR TAILS

This is . . . An icebreaker activity in which participants tell anecdotes about themselves—some true, some not.

The purpose is . . . For participants to learn some interesting facts about each other. This information may prompt small talk later.

Use this when . . .
➤ Individuals don't know each other very well.
➤ A new team is forming.
➤ Individuals know each other well and want to test that knowledge or learn even more about each other.

Materials you'll need . . .
➤ A coin and a paper cup.

Here's how . . .
1. Have the team sit around a table so that everyone can see each other.
2. The first participant starts by placing the coin face up or face down under the cup so that no one can see it.
3. If the participant placed the coin face up, the participant tells a TRUE story about himself or herself. If the participant placed the coin face down, he or she tells a story that is UNTRUE.
4. The group then tries to guess whether the story is true or untrue.

5. The participant lifts the cup to reveal the answer.
6. Repeat until every participant has had a chance to tell a story.

Ask these questions . . .

➤ How did you decide whether to tell a true story or not? *(My life is boring and I wanted to tell an exciting story; I knew no one would believe that this really happened; I'm no good at bluffing so I had to tell a true story.)*

➤ How did you determine if someone's story was true or not? *(I watched for long pauses in the story; If they had lots of detail I tended to believe them; I watched their eyes.)*

➤ If you made up a story, where did the story come from? *(It actually happened to my sister; It's something I wished had happened to me; It just seemed like Chuck would like this story.)*

➤ What's the value in getting to know each other outside a strict work setting?

➤ How can we learn more about each other back on the job?

Tips for success . . .

➤ Encourage everyone to make their stories short (you may even want to impose a time limit), so you can hear lots of them.

➤ Don't let the time spent on determining if the story was true or not drag out. The point is to get the stories out and have fun. Being able to guess which stories are true is secondary. Have a quick vote immediately after the story rather than asking everyone to comment on their vote.

Try these variations . . .

➤ If you don't have a cup, have the participants use their hand or a slip of paper to cover the coin.

➤ Limit the stories to workplace situations.

➤ For participants who know each other really well, have everyone tell a story about someone else rather than themselves. When voting on whether the story was true or not, the storyteller and the subject of the story don't vote.

➤ To speed things, have participants make a statement about themselves rather than tell a story. For example, "I've been to every state in the United States at least once." True or false?

For virtual teams . . . This activity works well regardless of the technology used.

1. Participants can send you an e-mail or voice mail to reveal whether the story is true or not.
2. If audio is not available, participants can e-mail their stories.

NOTE: please leave the line 2 as it was. They are not using email, they would be typing into a web conference.

HUMAN POKER

This is . . .   An icebreaker activity in which participants form good poker hands with cards handed to them at the beginning.

The purpose is . . .   For participants to have fun mingling and loosen up a bit and to increase the energy in the room.

Use this when . . .
- ➤ The group is large (more than 25 participants).
- ➤ Most people don't know each other.
- ➤ You don't have time for long introductions or icebreakers.
- ➤ You want a fun way to break a large group into teams of 5 members each.

Materials you'll need . . .
- ➤ A deck of playing cards for every 30–40 participants (use three to four decks for a group of 98 participants)—all decks shuffled and mixed together.

Here's how . . .
1. As participants enter the room, hand each one a randomly chosen playing card from the mixed decks.
2. Give participants 5–10 minutes (depending on the size of the group) to compare cards and form groups of five members to construct the best five-card poker hand they can.

For **example . . .**	Winning five-card poker hands in order from highest to lowest:

1. Royal Flush (10, J, Q, K, and Ace of the same suit).
2. Straight Flush (all five cards in sequence and of the same suit).
3. Four-of-a-Kind (four cards of equal rank).
4. Full House (three of equal rank with two different cards of equal rank).
5. Flush (any five cards of the same suit).
6. Straight (all five cards in sequence regardless of suit).
7. Three-of-a-Kind (three cards of equal rank).
8. Two Pair (two cards of equal rank with two different cards of equal rank).
9. Pair (two cards of equal rank).
10. High card (no pairs, the highest of the five cards determines strength).

Ask these **questions . . .**	➤ How did you decide which poker hand to pursue? *(I had a 9 and so did the person next to me when we started, so we figured we just needed two more; I don't know how to play poker, so I held up my card and waited for someone to grab me; As soon as I figured out there were more Queens in the room, I let go of the straight I was looking for and went after Queens.)*
	➤ Did anyone change teams after joining one? Why? How did it make the other team members feel? *(I did, but I felt guilty about it; She changed because they bribed her.)*
	➤ How much did the time limit factor into the game? *(We were going for a Royal Flush, but the time limit made us settle for a straight; We were done long before time was up, so we started trading players to go from a Full House to Four-of-a-Kind.)*

> How might you play the game differently if we did this again next week? What strategies did you learn that would improve your hand?

Tips for success . . .

> Don't worry about having too many decks of cards to play with. More is better than not enough (it allows teams to form "good" poker hands).
> You may want to award a small prize for the winning hand(s).
> For those not familiar with the rules, post the 10-item list of poker hands or pass them out on paper.
> You can make it easier to form good hands by using more decks and pulling out all the 2s, 3s, 4s, and 5s.
> Beforehand, decide whether participants can begin forming the poker hands as soon as they get their cards (as a reward for being early or on time) or whether they must wait until everyone is present so that everyone starts at the same time.
> If more than one deck is used, be prepared to handle a tie breaker (because it's now possible for two groups to get an identical Full House, for example).
> With multiple decks, be prepared for poker hands that are not possible with one deck (e.g., five Kings) and either outlaw them or include them in the hierarchy of winning hands that you post.

Try these variations . . .

> Use a different card game, such as gin rummy.
> Use this activity to divide large groups into teams of 5 for later work sessions, team-building exercises, brain-storming sessions, and so forth.
> For smaller groups, or to help a group just pair up, post four randomly chosen cards and play a version of Texas Hold'em. Participants pair up

with someone whose card, with theirs and those posted, create the best hand.

➤ Make the game easier (and quicker) by eliminating many of the winning poker hands. For example, ask people to get into teams of Four-of-a-Kind or a Flush.

➤ Hand each participant two cards. Participants can choose only ONE to play with (which may depend on what card others are looking for).

➤ Allow participants to select their cards. Don't let them talk with anyone or get cues from anyone already in the room before they select their card!

➤ Have a Round 2. Once all the poker hands are made, announce that everyone must get into another hand. No one can be in a hand with anyone they were with in Round 1. Did the poker hands get better (stronger?) or not?

For virtual teams . . .

This activity isn't suitable for virtual teams.

I AM . . .

This is . . . An icebreaker activity that can be a light and fun or a deep and serious way for participants to get to know each other better.

The purpose is . . . For participants to learn how the others perceive themselves.

Use this when . . .
- ➤ Individuals do not know each other very well.
- ➤ A new team is forming.
- ➤ One or more of the individuals are new to the team.

Materials you'll need . . .
- ➤ A large index card for each participant.
- ➤ A straight pin or a piece of tape for each participant.
- ➤ A pen or a pencil for each participant.

Here's how . . .
1. Have each participant write "I AM . . ." in large letters at the top of their card.
2. Ask participants to write five endings to the sentence that are true of themselves. Allow 3 minutes.
3. Have participants pin (or tape) the card to the front of their shirt.
4. Participants then mingle SILENTLY for 3 minutes to read each other's cards.
5. For another 6 minutes, participants converse, exploring the statements that they had read that intrigued them.

For **example . . .**	"I AM . . . 1. Outspoken. 2. Anxious for my trip to Hong Kong later this year! 3. A single father of three. 4. An amateur weightlifter. 5. Tired today after a very long weekend."

Ask these questions . . .

➤ Why is it important for us to know each other beyond a purely work-related context? *(We are more than just what we do for a living; Sometimes things outside work affect our work and it's good to be more understanding.)*

➤ How difficult (or easy) was it to share information about yourself? *(It was hard to put things about myself in that format of "I am"; I kept wanting to just put things about my family and nothing else.)*

➤ How can we learn more about each other back on the job?

Tips for success . . .

➤ Encourage participants to write the first things that come to mind rather than deliberating too long. First thoughts are usually the most telling and/or the most likely to prompt reactions and discussion from others.

➤ Don't allow more than a few minutes to fill in the cards for the reason above.

➤ You may want to share a few examples to show how simple this can be. Don't think too long and hard about your examples, either!

Try these variations . . .

➤ Use "I AM NOT . . ." for the title.
➤ Use "I AM PROUD OF . . ." for the title.
➤ Use "I HOPE . . ." for the title.
➤ Use "I FEAR . . ." for the title.
➤ Limit the statements to work-related responses.

- Collect the cards after the activity. At a later date, pull them out and see how many can properly identify the author of each card.
- Shorten the activity by skipping Step 4.
- Encourage discussion later by skipping Step 5.

For virtual teams . . .

This activity works well regardless of the technology used.

1. After Step 2, have participants read or type their answers to "I am . . ." for others to hear or read.
2. If one-on-one communication is not possible, facilitate Step 5 so that everyone gets a chance to explore with everyone else.
3. A variation: Have participants send in their answers ahead of time. Post or show the answers to the group and let them guess whose list is whose.

KIDS' STUFF

This is . . .	An icebreaker activity with several topics that take participants back to their childhood.
The purpose is . . .	To put the participants on a more level playing field reminiscent of childhood and have fun remembering "way back when."
Use this when . . .	➤ Participants do not know each other very well. ➤ One or more of the individuals are new to the team. ➤ You don't have prep time and/or materials for anything more elaborate.
Materials you'll need . . .	➤ No materials are necessary for this activity.
Here's how . . .	1. Have the group sit in a circle. 2. Ask the participants to introduce themselves (name, job, location, etc.). 3. As part of the introduction, participants also share what their favorite childhood toy was.
For example . . .	"Hi, I'm Lynn, a customer service rep from our Las Vegas facility. My favorite toy was those little troll dolls. My brother and I used to build little houses for them. We put in carpet, tile, homemade furniture and even had working lights hooked up to batteries! Heck, I think I still have a few of them in my attic."

Ask these questions . . .	➤ How difficult (or easy) was it to share information about yourself with the rest of us? *(It was fun talking about something that others my age could relate to; It's amazing how some toys are still popular today; This really brought me back and made me less anxious about the meeting coming up.)*
	➤ Why is it important to get to know each other beyond a purely work-related context?
Tips for success . . .	➤ Don't comment on people's responses other than to perhaps ask if they still have the toy or what happened to it. Commentary beyond that can make people want to try to impress you.
	➤ Go first so that others see how easy and unintimidating it can be to share childhood memories.
	➤ Something about going back to childhood puts everyone on a more level ground. This activity is particularly effective when people of different organizational levels need to work together as a team.
Try these variations . . .	➤ This is a good icebreaker for very large groups. If people aren't already in groups (at a round table, for example), have them get into groups of 5–10 people. Have them introduce themselves only within the smaller group. They won't know everyone in the room, but they'll at least know a few. Alternatively, give them 2 minutes to introduce themselves to as many people as they can in the room.
	➤ Other topics could be your favorite childhood _ Memory. _ Snack or treat. _ Birthday or Christmas present. _ Game.

_ Halloween costume.

_ Subject in school.

_ TV show or movie.

_ Meal.

_ Place to hang out.

➤ Other childhood topics could be

_ The person you admired most as a kid.

_ Your first job (when you were paid by someone other than your parents).

_ What you wanted to be when you grew up.

_ Your first crush.

_ Your first kiss.

_ Your first memory of any kind.

For virtual teams . . . This activity works well regardless of the technology used.

1. If audio is not available, participants can type in their stories.

PENNIES AND DICE

This is . . .   An icebreaker activity in which a penny and dice randomly dictate the kind of information participants will share.

The purpose is . . .   For participants to learn interesting facts or perspectives from each other while warming up for a meeting or training.

Use this when . . .
- ➤ Participants don't know each other very well.
- ➤ A new team is forming.
- ➤ The group needs to loosen up before a meeting or other gathering.

Materials you'll need . . .
- ➤ One penny.
- ➤ One die.
- ➤ One cup.
- ➤ A flip chart and marker (optional).

Here's how . . .
1. The team sits around a table so that everyone can see each other.
2. The first participant puts the penny and die in the cup, shakes them up, and shoots them out.
3. The participant then shares something personal according to whether the penny came up heads or tails and to what number showed up on the die (see the example below for guidelines).

4. The cup goes to the next participant, who shoots and shares accordingly.

For example . . .

Heads = Most favorite (thing about . . .).
Tails = Least favorite (thing about . . .).
1 = Your job.
2 = Your family.
3 = Your home.
4 = Your most recent vacation.
5 = Your personality.
6 = Your appearance.

Dean gets a heads and a 3. He would share his favorite thing about his home.
Cherie gets a tails and a 5. She would share her least favorite thing about her personality.

Ask these questions . . .

➤ How difficult was it for you to think of something to share? *(Easy, I love talking about my family; Not bad, as long as I didn't get a 5 or 6 and have to talk about myself; It was hard to talk about my home, because I prefer to be private.)*

➤ Were you hoping for a particular number or side of the penny? Why? *(I wanted to talk about my last vacation but couldn't throw a 4; I wanted to get heads, because I hate having to be negative about anything.)*

➤ What's the value in getting to know each other outside a strict work setting?

➤ How can we learn more about each other back on the job?

Tips for success . . .

➤ Pick a participant you know will feel comfortable sharing to go first and to set the tone for the rest of the group.

> ➤ Post the guidelines on the flip chart so that participants easily remember what to talk about when they shoot.
> ➤ For those who don't like what they get (heads/tails or the number), don't force the issue. Let them shoot again. It's more important for people to share willingly than to follow strict rules.

Try these variations . . .
> ➤ Skip the cup. Have one participant flip the coin for another, who throws the die and then shares accordingly.
> ➤ Explain the activity to the group and let them identify the six categories they want to discuss. For a "continuous improvement" discussion, have heads = *what you would change* and tails = *what you would keep the same* about six topics related to a project or work process.
> For a "project planning" discussion, have heads = *what success you want to have* and tails = *what pitfalls you want to avoid* for six elements of the project.

For virtual teams . . .
This activity works well regardless of the technology used. Just be sure each participant location has a penny, a die, and a cup. For variation . . .

1. You have the master penny, die, and cup, and you shoot for everyone.
2. You shoot the die, and participants flip their own penny (they are more likely to have a penny handy than a die).
3. The person who just shared a story shoots for the next participant.
4. Let the group choose the six categories.

SCRAMBLE

This is . . . A frantic activity in which participants simultaneously strategize and gather and summarize introductory information about each other and then present their findings to the group.

The purpose is . . . For participants to have fun learning more about each other as individuals and as a group at a somewhat hectic pace.

Use this when . . .
➤ The group is too large to have each person introduce himself or herself individually.
➤ You want to inject a lot of energy into the group.
➤ You don't have prep time and/or materials for anything more elaborate.

Materials you'll need . . .
➤ No materials are necessary for this activity.

Here's how . . .
1. Divide the group into teams of 3–9 participants.
2. Give each team a topic. (Be sure to have enough topics for the number of teams you create.)
3. Teams get 3 minutes to strategize how they will gather information about their topic from ALL the other participants in the room.
4. Teams get 3 minutes to gather information about their topic from each other (this happens simultaneously).
5. Teams get 3 minutes to summarize the data they collected.

6. Teams each get 1 minute to present their findings to the rest of the group.

For example . . .   Topics may be work related (number of years with company, office location, college degrees, job title, languages spoken, experience prior to coming here, etc.) or nonwork related (pets, birthplace, favorite ice cream flavor, number of kids, last vacation destination, hobbies, etc.).

Ask these questions . . .
- ➤ How did you accomplish your goals during each phase—what were your keys to success? *(We divided the room geographically to get the info; We planned who would get the info from who so we didn't bump into each other; We put all the info we gathered on this grid.)*
- ➤ How did you adjust your strategy once you started to implement? *(When I couldn't talk to Patrick, I pointed at him so that Alex could get him instead; We were lost, we didn't know what to do when they started picking us off one by one.)*
- ➤ During which phase did you feel the most rushed? Why?
- ➤ How does that relate to your approach to work—when do you feel most rushed?

Tips for success . . .
- ➤ Warn the group during their strategy phase that they will have only 3 minutes to gather all the information they need and that the other teams will be gathering information from them as well. It WILL be chaotic.
- ➤ Don't help the teams, especially when the mingling begins and the chaos ensues.
- ➤ Watch the time carefully. It's easy for the time to expand as the groups insist on more and more time to complete each phase. Resist.

Try these variations . . .

> Give the teams an extra minute or two to summarize their findings on a flip chart. Rather than make a presentation, post the charts and encourage everyone to review them all.
> For larger groups, give the same topic to more than one group (to speed up information gathering).
> For larger groups, have the teams gather sample data from a representative section of the group rather than from all participants.
> Give groups more time for the strategizing and summarizing steps. (The hysteria of gathering data in 3 minutes is a huge part of the fun, so resist the temptation to give more time there!)

For virtual teams . . .

This activity isn't suitable for virtual teams.

WORD COUNT

This is . . . An introduction activity that requires participants to introduce another participant in exactly 47 words—no more, no less.

The purpose is . . . Everyone will learn some interesting information about each other. This information may prompt some small talk later.

Use this when . . .
- ➤ Individuals do not know each other very well.
- ➤ A new team is forming.
- ➤ You don't have prep time and/or materials for anything more elaborate.

Materials you'll need . . .
- ➤ No materials are necessary for this activity.

Here's how . . .
1. Have the participants pair up.
2. Have them interview each other for 2 minutes each.
3. Allow 6 minutes for the participants to individually work out an introduction for their partner that is exactly 47 words long. No more, no less!
4. Have each participant then give his or her 47-word introduction.

For example . . . "This is Tim. He joined us over 11 years ago, after being with several other firms. His degree is from Ohio State, where he was in the marching band and became quite the Buckeye football fan (Go Bucks!). He started out functional but is now more technical."

Ask these questions . . .	➤ How much did you learn about each other? *(I learned a lot about those guys in the other building; I didn't learn much that I didn't already know; I learned stuff I never knew, and I've worked with her for years.)*
	➤ How difficult (or easy) was it to share information about yourself with your partner? *(Pretty easy to control how much I shared because of the limit of words; I told one thing only; It was hard to keep myself reigned in since I'm a pretty open person and love to share.)*
	➤ Was it more (or less) difficult to hear your information shared with the rest of the group? *(It didn't bother me at all; I liked not being the one to say it; I wanted to correct her when she said the name of my pet wrong.)*
	➤ How can we learn more about each other back on the job?
Tips for success . . .	➤ You may want to supply pens and paper so people can write (and edit!) the introductions to get the exact word count.
	➤ Mix the group up if some participants already know each other.
	➤ Ease participants' minds about the 47-word rule. Suggest ways to make it easier. For example, if a draft is 45 words so far, just add "the end" and you have the magic 47.
Try these variations . . .	➤ Don't allow time to plan. Just talk. Have the group count the words until 47, at which time the person must stop talking, even if midsentence.
	➤ Use a different number than 47—especially if there a number that is significant for the group or the organization.

➤ Allow the partnerships to work on both introductions together (at Step 3).
➤ Skip the partnerships and just have each individual work out a self-introduction, keeping to the 47-word number requirement.
➤ Require that certain content be part of the introduction (His or her experience on this kind of project? Greatest strength in his or her field? His or her philosophy on improving customer service?).
➤ Have everyone write a 47-word self-introduction on an index card but leave their name off. Shuffle the cards and start to read them. See how many words you have to read before the group accurately guesses whose card you are reading.

For virtual teams . . .
This activity works well for groups that are able to communicate via instant messaging, e-mail, or telephone.
1. After Step 1, have the participants connect via instant messaging, e-mail, or telephone to accomplish Step 2 (and maybe Step 3 if they work together on crafting the 47-word introduction).
2. Everyone reconvenes for Step 4.
3. A variation: Assign pairs before the meeting, and have partners do Steps 1–3 beforehand.
4. A variation: Have each participant write his or her own 47-word introduction and forward it to you beforehand. Read (or type) them to the group. See how many words you have to read or type before the group guesses whose introduction you are reading.
5. Each of the other variations listed above can work for a virtual team using this activity.

CHAPTER 4

Battling: Games That Teach Healthy Competition

 **BALLOON BATTLE**

This is . . .   A game in which two teams see how many times they can get a balloon to touch their opponent's wall while they remain stationary.

The purpose is . . .   To energize the group and develop planning and strategy skills.

Use this when . . .
- The group is low energy and needs a pick-me-up.
- Individuals are facing a task or project that will require them to use strategy and planning skills.
- Individuals struggle with anticipating and then adjusting for potential roadblocks to their original plans.

Materials you'll need . . .   Four inflated balloons.

Here's how . . .
1. Divide the group into two teams of roughly equal size.
2. Designate opposite walls as the goals for each team.
3. Explain that each team's objective is to outscore the other team. One point is awarded for each time a balloon touches the opponent's wall.
4. Once players position themselves, they will not be allowed to move—they must remain stationary.
5. Give the teams 3 minutes to strategize where they will position themselves.
6. Have the teams move into these positions.

7. Give two balloons to each team.

8. Give the signal to begin playing.

9. Keep score for 6 minutes, and then call the end of the game.

Ask these questions . . .

➤ How did you do at scoring points? *(Going to Brad each time was good since he had no defender on him; We had to always aim high to get over their line of defenders.)*

➤ How did you do at defending points? *(We put too many people on offense; We were spaced just right to defend everything but down past Lisa; We didn't realize how much more important defense would be than offense.)*

➤ Did you adjust your position strategy when you saw the other team placing themselves? How? *(We held to our original plan and failed; We didn't expect them to stand like that so we moved two more people on defense; We realized offense was more important and more difficult so we had to change a few roles.)*

➤ What did you learn about your placement strategy as the game played? *(It's more about defense than offense, so we were not positioned well; We should have passed more.)*

➤ How does what we did here apply to our work back on the job?

Tips for success . . .

➤ Although each team starts with two balloons, there is nothing special about the balloons. Whenever *any* balloon touches a wall, a point is awarded.

➤ Have extra balloons for the inevitable breaking!

➤ Announce one of these rules before play begins: After you score a point, the balloon must touch an opponent before you can score again. (This prevents a team player from holding a balloon next to the wall and touching it a million times in a row.) After you score a point, the balloon must cross the middle of the room before you can score again.

➤ Think through beforehand how to deal with balloons that go out of reach. Will you throw them back into play? Will they be out of play for the rest of the game? Announce the rule before play begins.

Try these variations . . .
➤ Use only one balloon at a time.
➤ Use some kind of (soft!) ball.
➤ Use extra large balloons or long, skinny circus balloons.
➤ Allow players to move one foot as long as their other foot stays planted at all times.
➤ In a small room, or if there are many players, blindfold some or all of the players.
➤ For the fiercely competitive, as well as for those wanting to focus on continuous improvement, add a Round 2. After Round 1, give the teams 2 minutes to regroup and restrategize, and then play again.
➤ See how well the teams adapt to change: After they have positioned themselves for play, announce that the walls used for each team's goals are reversed. This will put those intended for defense on offense and vise versa.

For virtual teams . . .
This activity isn't suitable for virtual teams.

 # CHOPSTICKS

This is . . .	A relay race in which teams move an ice cube in and out of a cup using only a pair of chopsticks.
The purpose is . . .	For participants to learn teamwork and supportive behaviors.
Use this when . . .	➤ Participants are not as supportive of each other as they should be.
	➤ The group needs to focus on rallying behind each other.
	➤ Participants need to deal with pressure from their peers.
Materials you'll need . . .	➤ A cup for each team.
	➤ At least one ice cube for each team.
	➤ A pair of chopsticks for each team.
Here's how . . .	1. Divide the group into teams of 3–7 members each.
	2. Give each team a cup with an ice cube in it and a pair of chopsticks.
	3. The first person on the team must remove the ice cube from the cup and place it on the table, using only the chopsticks.
	4. The next person must put the ice cube back into the cup, using only the chopsticks.
	5. Keep alternating until every team member has moved the ice cube into or out of the cup.
	6. The first team to finish the moves wins.

Ask these	➤ How did you move the ice cube quickly? *(Pressing*
questions . . .	*the ice cube against the cup helped; Clamping down at*
	the same spot wore a groove in the cube for us.)

➤ What kept you from being even faster? *(Everyone yelling at me to hurry made me drop it several times in a row; Knowing I was the last one added to my pressure; I've never used chopsticks before.)*

➤ How did your teammates affect your success when you had the chopsticks? *(They encouraged me even after I dropped the ice cube on the floor; They gave me tips on what worked for them.)*

➤ How did they impact your sense of pressure? *(He kept rushing everyone; She calmed us all down; He made us feel good even if we dropped the ice cube.)*

➤ How do your teammates affect your performance on the job? How can they better help you?

➤ How can you better influence your teammates on the job?

Tips for
success . . .

➤ Inexpensive, disposable wooden chopsticks make the task slightly easier than the lacquered Japanese sticks—both are available at Asian markets.

➤ Use cups that are large (more than 8 oz.) or even small bowls.

➤ Decide how to handle ice cubes dropped on the floor. Can participants pick them up by hands, or must they use the chopsticks? Announce the rule before play begins.

➤ If the teams do not have exactly the same number of people, declare up front how many times the ice cube must go in and out of the cup. This makes the game fair for all teams (smaller teams will have someone go twice to match the larger teams).

➤ For highly competitive groups, you may have to state up front that moving the cup at all (tipping it over, etc.) is not allowed.

Try these variations . . .	➤ Make it even more difficult by requiring participants to use their nondominant hand (those who are right-handed must use the left hand and vice versa).
	➤ Make it even more difficult by requiring that they do this blindfolded.
	➤ Make it even more difficult by requiring that two people work together—each one holding only one chopstick.
	➤ Have a second cup for each team located several feet away from the first one. Rather than just take the ice cube out, take it out and put it in the other cup.

For virtual teams . . .

This activity works well with virtual teams when the number of participants at each location is roughly the same.

1. Make sure each location has a set of materials.
2. Follow Steps 3–6 above. You will have to trust each location to be honest about the true finish time.
3. Be aware that while this activity may pull the participants in each location together, it may also foster their competitiveness with other locations.

COTTON BALLS

This is . . .　A relay race in which team members are blindfolded and try to move cotton balls from one end of the room to the other on a spoon.

The purpose is . . .　For participants to learn teamwork and communication skills as well as how to encourage each other when the pressure is on.

Use this when . . .
- ➤ The group needs to communicate and support each other better.
- ➤ Participants aren't depending on each other to be successful as much as they should.
- ➤ The group needs a shot of competitiveness to energize it.

Materials you'll need . . .
- ➤ Two large bowls for each team.
- ➤ A bag of cotton balls for each team.
- ➤ A large spoon for each team.
- ➤ One blindfold for each team.

Here's how . . .
1. Divide the group into teams of 3–7 members each.
2. Place one bowl for each team on a table on one side of the room and corresponding bowls across the room. Fill bowls on one side of the room with an equal number of cotton balls. This is the starting point for the teams.
3. Line each team up behind its bowl.
4. Blindfold the first person in each line.
5. Their task is to scoop up as many cotton balls as

possible with the spoon, take them across the room, and drop them into the other bowl. Their other hands must remain behind their backs at all times.

6. As soon as they are done, remove the blindfold and give it and the spoon to the next person on the team to continue the relay.

7. The game ends when all team members have had their turn. Teams count how many cotton balls they moved. Alternatively, teams may keep going until one team gets all its cotton balls moved.

Ask these questions . . .

➤ What was your strategy? *(Just let our teammate go, whether he or she had a lot of cotton balls or not; Take the time to get a big load of cotton balls before moving.)*

➤ How did you adjust your strategy as the game continued? *(We had to speed things up and just let some cotton balls fall; We had to guide each other much more than we expected.)*

➤ How did you feel when you saw how many cotton balls you had actually moved? *(I was disappointed; I thought I had more than that; I couldn't believe my teammates let me carry so few.)*

➤ How did your teammates' input affect your performance? *(I just tuned out their screaming; I wouldn't have gotten any cotton balls without their guidance; I needed to be reassured that I was doing well since I couldn't see.)*

➤ How does your teammates' input affect you on the job? How open are you to that input?

➤ How can you better influence your teammates on the job?

Tips for success . . .

➤ Encourage team members to verbally help the blindfolded one ("No, you don't have any cotton balls yet, scoop again!").

> Make a rule about what to do with cotton balls that fall in transit. May another teammate retrieve them and put them back in the starting bowl? Are the dropped cotton balls lost for the rest of the game? May the blindfolded one try to pick them up? Announce the rule before play begins.

> Be careful about spacing the bowls. Place them close together if you want the blindfolded participants bumping into each other. Space them further apart if you want them to be more autonomous.

> Have extra blindfolds so that the next person in line can be getting the blindfold on and be ready to move as soon as the one before hands off the spoon.

Try these variations . . .

> You may limit the number of trips the team can make from bowl to bowl. This means some will never be blindfolded, they but can act as coaches or helpers to those who are. Each trip will take on greater importance. What kind of teamwork happens then?

> Eliminate the blindfolds. Instead, players may not use their hands at all (e.g., they hold the spoons in their mouths or in the crooks of their elbows). Alternatively, two participants must hold the spoon between the backs of their hands or their forearms.

> Have them walk backward.

For virtual teams . . .

This activity isn't suitable for virtual teams.

HIGHER LOWER

This is . . .	A dice game in which participants try to guess whether they will roll a number higher or lower than the one rolled immediately before them.
The purpose is . . .	For participants to get energized while learning that sometimes things outside their control can impact their best efforts.
Use this when . . .	➤ You need to inject some energy into the group. ➤ Individuals are blaming each other unnecessarily. ➤ The group needs to remember some things are out of its control.
Materials you'll need . . .	➤ A pair of dice for each team.
Here's how . . .	1. Divide the group into teams of 4–6 members. 2. Each team gets a pair of dice. 3. The first player rolls the dice. 4. The next player then predicts if he or she will roll a number higher or lower than the previous player. Predicting that the same number as the previous player's will come up is not an option. 5. The player then rolls the dice. 6. One point is awarded for a correct guess. No point is awarded for an incorrect guess. 7. The next player makes his or her prediction, and play continues around the circle until time is up. 8. The player with the most points wins.

For example . . .	Rachel rolls a 7. Adam predicts he'll roll lower (than 7) and rolls a 3. He gets 1 point. Sara predicts she'll roll higher (than 3) and rolls a 10. She gets 1 point. Matt predicts he'll roll lower (than 10) and rolls an 8. He gets 1 point. Miriam predicts she'll roll lower (than 8) and rolls an 8. She doesn't get a point. Rachel predicts she'll roll lower (than 8) and rolls a 12. She doesn't get a point.
Ask these questions . . .	➤ What strategies did you use? *(I went with "lower" for numbers above 6 and "higher" for numbers below 6; I just flipped back and forth no matter what number was showing; I followed his lead.)* ➤ How did you feel when you guessed wrong? *(Frustrated that I didn't get a point; No big deal, it's just a game; Annoyed that the game is so dependent on luck; OK until they laughed at me for not getting points again.)* ➤ How did you feel when others guessed right and moved ahead of you? *(A little ticked that they were lucky and I wasn't; Happy for them; Fine until they started gloating.)* ➤ How did you feel when you rolled the same but weren't allowed to have called it? *(Like the game was unfair; It was frustrating, because once I was sure I'd roll the same number and I did, but I couldn't get credit for it.)* ➤ How is this game similar to situations we have back on the job?
Tips for success . . .	➤ Because players are not allowed to predict the same number (it was not higher or lower as he or she had predicted!) the frustration level can build, prompting good discussion during the Debrief.

➤ This game is based entirely on luck. Watch carefully for reactions so you can help prompt discussion during the Debrief if necessary.

Try these variations . . .

➤ Have participants lose a point if they roll the same number as the person before them. (Yes, this isn't "fair." One more thing to discuss afterwards!)

➤ Allow players to predict higher, lower, or the same. Give double points if someone predicts "the same" and then rolls it.

➤ Have points awarded to the team, not the individual, and the teams compete against each other. Team members will then give input on whether one's prediction should be higher or lower. People may get angry if their prediction isn't accepted and then indignant if it is correct.

➤ Use only one die. This will increase the likelihood of "the same" coming up and make predicting even more difficult.

➤ Use a deck of cards instead of dice.

For virtual teams . . .

This activity works well regardless of the technology used.

1. For smaller virtual teams, play together instead of in teams. Have one person roll the dice for each participant regardless of their location. Listen for participants blaming the dice roller for bad throws, and discuss this during the Debrief. If there is no video, call out the results of each throw. Follow the steps above.

2. For virtual teams in which the number of participants at each location is roughly the same, each location can be a team. Make sure each location has a set of dice.

3. Follow the rest of the steps above. You will have to trust each location to be honest about results.

4. Be aware that while this activity may pull the participants in each location together, it may also foster their competitiveness with other locations.

MARSHMALLOW DODGE BALL

This is . . .   A version of dodge ball played indoors using marshmallows instead of balls.

The purpose   For participants to learn to cooperate as a team in a
is . . .   high-pressure, fast-paced environment.

Use this   ➤ The pace at your organization is very fast and re-
when . . .   quires quick adjustments to strategies and tactics.
   ➤ Individuals are being too independent and not
   relying on their teammates enough.
   ➤ The group needs a boost of energy and fun.

Materials   ➤ A bag of large marshmallows.
you'll need . . . ➤ Masking tape.

Here's   1. Divide the group in two, and give each team half a
how . . .   bag of marshmallows.
   2. Divide the play area in half, and mark the dividing
   line with a piece of tape. Teams each take a side of
   the line.
   3. On your signal, participants throw marshmallows
   at the members of the opposite team.
   4. They can throw only one marshmallow at a time
   and only with the same hand each time.
   5. If they are hit with a marshmallow, they are "out"
   and must go to the side of the play area and wait
   their turn to reenter play.

6. If they catch a marshmallow, the person who threw it is out AND a member of the team that caught the marshmallow and is waiting on the sideline may now reenter.
7. The winning team eliminates the other team completely.

Ask these questions . . .

> What was your strategy for success? *(We kept the good players up front; We played defense—catching marshmallows—as our offense.)*
> How did you change strategy as the game progressed? *(When we lost our two best players, the rest of us had to get more aggressive; We found we weren't very good at catching, so we had to throw more accurately; I ducked behind these two guys most the time.)*
> How much did you have to depend on your teammates? *(If it weren't for Caroline, I'd have been out two or three times; I think they depended on me to keep catching the marshmallows more than I depended on them.)*
> How is this game similar to our jobs?
> What can we learn from this activity that will help us in our jobs?

Tips for success . . .

> If there are concerns about some players being more skilled than others, handicap them by forcing them to throw underhand or with their non-dominant arm.
> Encourage those who claim they aren't very good at catching or throwing.
> For very competitive groups, you may want to designate that players can throw only with their nondominant arm.
> For very competitive groups, divide the marshmallows in half by counting them, don't just eyeball it.

Try these
variations . . .

➤ Use under-filled water balloons (outside!) instead of marshmallows.

➤ Use very light foam balls instead of marshmallows.

➤ Make the game easier by not requiring the marshmallows be caught but merely deflected with a hand in order to free a teammate and put the thrower of the marshmallow out.

➤ Eliminate the rule that only one marshmallow can be thrown at a time.

➤ Designate more specifically where the marshmallow must hit or not hit on the person for it to count (e.g., no hits above the neck or hits only on exposed flesh count).

➤ Separate the teams by a "no man's land." Instead of a line down the center of the play area, make a strip 5–15 feet wide. No one can enter this area. This will make the throwing accuracy more critical (and may help reduce the power with which marshmallows hit participants).

➤ Have the teams make each other s'mores afterward with the marshmallows they collected (just kidding!).

For virtual
teams . . .

This activity isn't suitable for virtual teams.

SNAKE EYES

This is . . .   A dice rolling game in which points are awarded for 1s, but points stop accumulating temporarily when snake eyes is thrown.

The purpose is . . .   For participants to encourage teammates while learning to deal with temporary short- or long-term setbacks.

Use this when . . .
- Individuals are acting more like individuals than like a team.
- The group is blaming each other for setbacks.
- The group needs to remember some things are out of one's control.

Materials you'll need . . .
- A pair of dice for each team.
- A small prize for the winning team (optional).

Here's how . . .
1. Divide the group into teams of 4–6 members.
2. Give each team a pair of dice.
3. Team members take turns throwing both the dice.
4. When a player rolls a 1, the team gets 1 point and that player rolls again.
5. When a player doesn't roll a 1, the dice go to the next player to roll.
6. When a player rolls two 1s at once ("snake eyes"), no point is awarded, and this player's turn is over.
7. After snake eyes is rolled, play continues but no points are awarded for any 1's until someone rolls

snake eyes again. When this happens, the team gets 2 points, and this player gets to roll again.

8. Repeat Steps 4–7 for 5 minutes.

9. The team with the most points after 5 minutes is the winner.

For example . . .

Jon rolls a 1. The team gets 1 point.

Jon rolls another 1. The team gets another point (and now has 2 points).

Jon doesn't roll another 1; the dice go to Sue. The team still has 2 points.

Sue doesn't roll a 1; the dice go to Laura. The team still has 2 points.

Laura rolls snake eyes; the dice go to Akiko. The team still has 2 points.

Akiko rolls a 1. The team doesn't get a point and still has 2 points.

Akiko doesn't roll a 1; the dice go to Mario. The team still has 2 points.

Mario rolls snake eyes. The team gets 2 points. The team now has 4 points.

Mario then rolls a 1. The team gets 1 point. The team now has 5 points.

Ask these questions . . .

➤ How did you feel when you got a 1? (*I was relieved that I got to help the cause; I was disappointed it took so long for me to gain a point for us; Happy I got one first.*)

➤ How did you feel when someone else got a 1? (*I was excited for her; I was a little disappointed that I was the only one now who hadn't made any points for the team; Glad we were getting points.*)

➤ How did you feel when you got snake eyes? (*I was embarrassed; I was afraid the others would be mad at me; I was excited to finally break the ban on points we had going from the last snake eyes that she had rolled so long ago.*)

> How did you feel when someone else got snake eyes? *(Frustrated that we were going so well and then stopped getting points; Excited that she broke the ban on points; Relieved it wasn't me who stopped the points for us.)*

> How similar are these feelings to your own successes and failures, as well as the successes and failures of your teammates?

Tips for success . . .

> Walk through an extended example (see above) to make sure the rules are clear to everyone.

> Stay close to the teams as they start. They're likely to still have questions about the rules as they start to roll the dice.

> It's best to have someone on the team designated Scorekeeper.

Try these variations . . .

> Compete to see which team can get a set number of points (100?) first.

> Create different penalties for the dice that impact others (to reinforce shared responsibility and teamwork). For example, when you roll a 6, the person to your left must sing 6 notes from a popular song; when you roll a 2 the person to your right must give 2 reasons why they love working here that have not been stated yet.

> Play with cards instead of dice. Let face cards represent what the 1s did. Shuffle the deck. To play, participants draw from anywhere in the deck (without peaking, of course). One face card warrants 1 point, and two face cards are snake eyes!

For virtual teams . . .

This activity works well regardless of the technology used.

1. For smaller virtual groups, do not break into teams. Have one person roll the dice for each participant, regardless of their location. Listen for

participants blaming the dice roller for bad throws, and discuss this during the Debrief. Alternatively, make sure each participant has a pair of dice. If there is no video, call out the results of each throw. Then follow the steps above.

2. For virtual groups in which the number of participants at each location is roughly the same, each location can be a team. Make sure each group has a pair of dice.

3. Follow the rest of the steps above. You will have to trust each location to be honest about the results.

4. Be aware that while this activity may pull the participants in each location together, it may also foster their competitiveness with other locations.

TABLECLOTH

This is . . .	An activity in which participants collectively try to turn a tablecloth over using only their feet.
The purpose is . . .	For participants to learn to work together for a solution they all must implement together.
Use this when . . .	➤ The group is not cooperating with each other as well as they should. ➤ The group needs to loosen up, have some fun, and laugh. ➤ Creative problem solving is not happening enough.
Materials you'll need . . .	➤ One flannel–backed round or square tablecloth per team.
Here's how . . .	1. If the group has more than 10–12 people, divide them into teams of 6–12 participants each. 2. Have the teams lie on their backs in a circle with their feet in the center. 3. Once they are situated, have them raise their feet. 4. Drape the tablecloth over their feet so that the flannel side is facing down. 5. Challenge them to turn the tablecloth over completely so that the flannel side is facing up, using only their feet. 6. Give them 5 minutes to do this. 7. If the tablecloth falls off their feet, place it back on for them exactly as you did to start them off (no

matter how close they were to completing the task before they dropped the tablecloth).

<table>
<tr>
<td>

Ask these questions . . .

</td>
<td>

➤ What strategies worked for you to get the table-cloth flipped over? *(Talking through our plan before starting anything; Starting at that side first; All kicking hard at the same time.)*

➤ What other strategies did you try but didn't work? *(Trying to kick it up in the air and flip it midair; Depending too much on the ones with longer legs; We tried to roll it over starting at one corner.)*

➤ How did you feel when I first told you what the task was? *(I thought it was impossible; I thought you were kidding; I was energized and anxious to go at it.)*

➤ How often do you feel that way when work tasks are assigned to you?

➤ What can we take from our experience here that will help us back on the job?

</td>
</tr>
<tr>
<td>

Tips for success . . .

</td>
<td>

➤ Because participants get in such awkward positions, you may want to ask everyone to wear pants to work that day or otherwise warn them ahead of time about appropriate attire.

➤ Make sure they realize that their hands or arms may not touch the tablecloth.

➤ Don't give them ideas on how to accomplish the task, but do encourage them as they try different options.

➤ Once they understand the challenge and see the size of the tablecloth, allow them to shift their body positions if they choose. They may want to tighten or loosen their circle.

</td>
</tr>
<tr>
<td>

Try these variations . . .

</td>
<td>

➤ Have the participants sit in a circle, backs facing the center. Raise their hands overhead and make fists. Have them turn the tablecloth over without

</td>
</tr>
</table>

opening their fists. You may want to have them wear socks so their thumbs are neutralized.

➤ Use a rectangular tablecloth and see how the oblong shape affects the dynamics of who feels their effort is more or less difficult.

➤ Blindfold one or more members to make the task more difficult.

➤ Make the task easier by placing a mark at one point on the tablecloth. Instead of turning it over, the team must move that point around in a circle until it gets back to the place it started.

For virtual teams . . .

This activity works well with virtual teams in which the number of participants at each location is roughly the same.

1. Make sure each location has a tablecloth.
2. Follow the rest of the steps above. You will have to trust each location to be honest about the true finish time.
3. Be aware that while this activity may pull the participants in each location together, it may also foster their competitiveness with other locations.

TALL TOWERS

This is . . .	An activity in which teams work to build the tallest tower they can with small, flat objects.
The purpose is . . .	For participants to learn to work together toward a common goal.
Use this when . . .	➤ Individuals are being too independent and not relying on their teammates enough. ➤ Creative problem solving is not happening enough. ➤ The group is not cooperating as effectively as it could.
Materials you'll need . . .	➤ An assortment of objects from around the office for each team. ➤ A ruler or a tape measure. ➤ A small prize for the winning team (optional).
Here's how . . .	1. Divide the group into teams of 3–6 members each. 2. Teams are to build the tallest tower they can by stacking their items one on top of the other in order. 3. Each team member takes a turn choosing an item and adding it to the stack. 4. If the stack tumbles, the team must start over. 5. The team with the tallest standing tower at the end of 5 minutes is the winner.
For example . . .	Appropriate objects include sticky notepads, erasers, pencils, plastic cup lids, staplers, books, cell phones,

rolls of tape, paper clips, markers, and staple removers. Err on the side of having too many objects rather than too few.

Ask these questions . . .

➤ How did your team get as high as it did? *(We started with these pieces first to build a strong base; We used the thickest pieces first; We turned these things on their side.)*

➤ What unique ways did you find to make your tower taller with the objects given? *(We propped the pencils up like this; We opened the stapler and leaned it like this.)*

➤ What strategy did your team use to build? *(Thomas was our architect and told each of us what object to use and where to put it; We trusted each person to make a good decision on which object to add.)*

➤ How did you feel when others helped you or told you what to place or how to place it? *(It frustrated me; I loved the help; I wanted to do it myself; I didn't want to cross anyone.)*

➤ How did you feel when you caused the tower to fall? *(Embarrassed; Sad that I had let the team down; I didn't care, because I knew we had plenty of time; It wasn't my fault, the person before me put a pencil on wrong.)*

➤ How did you feel when someone else caused the tower to fall? *(I was a little mad; No big deal; Frustrated because we didn't have much time left.)*

➤ What does this activity tell you about working together?

➤ What can we take from this activity and apply to our jobs?

Tips for success . . .

➤ Watch the teams as they build so that you can comment later. Often they will take one of two extremes. Sometimes one master builder emerges and tells everyone what object to use, where to place it, and so forth. Alternatively, everyone stands back completely, and it's up the person on the spot to figure out what to do next.

➤ You may want to announce up front whether items can be used in ways other than to merely stack. You may also choose to see how many teams get creative about the use of the materials. For example, if you provide sticky notes, can they also be used to hold things together and add stability to the tower?

Try these variations . . .

➤ Tighten the rules by not allowing a team to re-build if the tower falls. This will put more emphasis (and stress!) on each placement of an object.

➤ Eliminate the rule that team members must take turns making a placement. If you do this, be prepared for one or two members to become builders while others sit back and watch or advise. In the Debrief, ask about these dynamics.

➤ Rather than a tower, have the teams build the highest arch.

➤ Have the teams choose a team leader who will direct them but who cannot place anything on the tower.

For virtual teams . . .

This activity works well with virtual teams in which the number of participants at each location is roughly the same.

1. Make sure each location has a set of materials.

2. Follow the rest of the steps above. You will have to trust each location to be honest about the finish height.

3. Be aware that while this activity may pull the participants in each location together, it may also foster their competitiveness with other locations.

TEAM SCORES

This is . . .   An indoor basketball game in which more points are
scored when more team members make a basket.

The purpose   For participants to learn to encourage others to
is . . .   contribute and be involved.

Use this
when . . .
- Individuals are negating the contributions of
  others on a team.
- The group needs to help all its members be successful and not always rely on a few to carry the
  rest.
- The group needs a shot of competitiveness to
  energize it.

Materials
you'll need . . .
- Two trashcans of equal size.
- Two bean bags, Koosh® balls, foam balls, or other
  similar items.

Here's
how . . .
1. Place the trashcans at opposite sides of the room.
2. Arrange the chairs in between the baskets. Half
   the chairs should be facing one trashcan, half
   facing the other. Space the chairs randomly
   throughout the room, though. Have everyone
   sit in a chair.
3. As in basketball, teams must get balls into the
   can in order to score. Designate which team is
   shooting for which can.
4. Participants cannot leave their seats during play,
   with one exception.

5. The exception is that one person may leave his or her chair temporarily to be a Rover. While out of his or her chair, the Rover cannot move with the ball (the ball can be thrown to and by the Rover, but the Rover cannot travel with it). The Rover can also retrieve balls that are out of reach (walk to it, pick it up, then throw it back into play). The Rover must sit down after he or she touches a ball once.

6. Each team can decide who and when any of them is the Rover. The role must change throughout the game (the same person cannot stand at the basket and have balls thrown to him or her to just drop in).

7. Either team can score with either ball—both of which are in play simultaneously.

8. After a basket is made, a Rover from the team that did NOT score must retrieve the ball. (The Rover will go to the basket, pull the ball out, and pass it to someone on his or her team to put the ball back into play.)

9. Interceptions and blocked passes are entirely legal (and encouraged!).

10. Scoring: The first time an individual on the team makes a basket, the team gets 1 point. The second time that the same person makes a basket, it is worth 3 points. The third time, 6 points. Every basket he or she makes after that is worth only 1 point.

For example . . . Team A is composed of Kiki, Suzanne, Rudy, Margie, Michael, and Jane. Jane scores first, and Team A has 1 point. Rudy scores next and gets 1 point (Team A has 2 points). Then Margie scores 1 point (Team A has 3). Then Jane scores again, and she gets 3 points (Team A has 6 points). Jane scores again and gets

6 points (team A has 12 points). Now, any more scores from Jane are worth only 1 point, but if Rudy or Margie scores again, theirs will be worth 3 points.

<table>
<tr><td>Ask these questions . . .</td><td>

➤ What was your strategy for scoring points? *(We wanted everyone to score a point first and then for everyone to score 3; We wanted one person to score the 1, 3, and 6 before someone else got their first 1.)*

➤ How did your strategy change as you played? *(We found scoring points for those who couldn't shoot well was easier if they were the Rover at the time; We stopped passing because we didn't catch well.)*

➤ How did you feel when everyone else had scored points but you? *(Like I was a drag on my team; I wasn't contributing enough; Happy that I had assisted many of them in scoring.)*

➤ Those of you who felt less skilled at basketball than others, how did it feel to have your team-mates encouraging you and cheering you on to make baskets? *(It was a real high for me; I am so used to being left out of sporting events, this was actually fun; Like I was really a part of the team, not just someone assigned to take a spot.)*

➤ How do we sometimes tend to hog the spotlight or keep others from "scoring" back on the job?

➤ How can we promote a stronger "all for one and one for all" atmosphere around here?

</td></tr>
<tr><td>Tips for success . . .</td><td>

➤ Keeping score can be confusing. This may be a good job for an extra participant if there is an uneven number. You may want to designate one person from each team to keep score (and not play) for the opposite team. It's best if you can make the score visible (white board, flip chart).

➤ Note that the scoring encourages everyone on a team to make a few baskets rather than one or two

</td></tr>
</table>

superstars, so don't change the scoring to make it simpler unless you want to lose that lesson of the activity.

➤ If the scoring gets too easy, move the baskets during the game to another location in the room (not unlike your workplace, where goals and objectives are constantly changing!).

➤ There will be a tendency to stretch to reach a ball, or to hop up briefly to catch or deflect a pass, so remind the group that their seat must stay in the chair. You may have to be a referee on that one. Impose a 3-point penalty for anyone caught leaving his or her chair illegally.

Try these variations . . .

➤ Apply this scoring system to almost any other game or contest—real basketball, soccer, lacrosse, card games, board games, and so forth.

➤ Use only one ball at a time (at least to begin) for less chaos. Alternatively, use more balls for more chaos!

➤ Explain the rules and have the teams design where they want their chairs to be placed. Afterward, explore their placement strategy.

➤ Make the role of Rover a permanent role. Before play begins, each team chooses only one person to be a Rover. This Rover does not get a chair. No one else can move off his or her chair at any time for any reason.

For virtual teams . . .

This activity isn't suitable for virtual teams.

UNSHUFFLE

This is . . .   A game in which participants try to organize a deck of cards, but one of them is out to sabotage their efforts.

The purpose is . . .   For participants to learn how destructive lack of trust can be to a team.

Use this when . . .
➤ The group is newly formed.
➤ Group members do not trust each other.
➤ The group is showing signs of paranoia.

Materials you'll need . . .
➤ A deck of cards for each team, shuffled well.
➤ A blank index card for each participant, folded in half and then in half again.
➤ An extravagant prize (which will be shown, but not awarded—optional).

Here's how . . .
1. Divide the group into teams of 5–7 members.
2. Explain that you will distribute an index card to each participant. Announce that one of the cards for each team will have a star on it, and the rest will be blank.
3. The job of the person who gets the star is to sabotage the team's efforts without getting caught. If the saboteurs succeed, they will get a prize (hold up the elaborate prize).
4. Distribute all the index cards (none of which has a star).

5. Give the teams 8 minutes to plan how they will put their shuffled deck of cards back in order as fast as possible.
6. Give each team a deck of shuffled cards and have them begin.
7. Record their times.
8. Have each team try to determine who the saboteur was.
9. After some accusations and discussion, reveal that no one was a saboteur.

Ask these questions . . .
➤ How did you feel working together, knowing that someone was trying to sabotage you? *(I was on my guard; I was watching for clues of who it would be; I was less engaged.)*
➤ How did you decide who was the saboteur? *(I was watching for someone to disagree a lot; He kept asking questions to stall us; She dropped cards more than once.)*
➤ How did you feel when someone accused you of being the saboteur? *(It hurt my feelings; It made me angry; I trust that person less now.)*
➤ How often do you believe others who tell you there is a saboteur?
➤ How does distrusting teammates affect your success?
➤ What implication does this activity have for us back on the job?

Tips for success . . .
➤ Don't put a star on any of the cards; leave them all blank. The point is to show how damaging paranoia and mistrust can be when there's clearly no one trying to do you in.
➤ As you distribute the index cards, make a show (this is all an act!) of being careful that the cards are not mixed up, so the group thinks one for each team really does have a star.

> Be explicit on how the finished deck of cards must look—Ace through King for each suit, but which suit should come first, second, third, and last? It may help to post the exact order for everyone to see.
> Don't hand out the shuffled decks until after the 8–minute planning period. Paranoia usually manifests most during this period.
> Show the prize for the saboteur and talk it up so that people are especially keen on catching the culprit.

Try these variations . . .
> Give index cards to some but not all of the teams. Compare the times of those who knew they didn't have a saboteur with the times of those who thought they did (but still didn't).
> Actually put a star a card. Compare the times of those teams with saboteurs versus those without. Which had a greater impact on the team's performance, having a saboteur or merely believing one was there? If you do this, don't put out a huge prize unless you're willing to part with it!
> Repeat the activity without any threat of sabotage. Note the differences in times.

For virtual teams . . .
This activity works well with virtual teams in which the number of participants at each location is roughly the same.
1. Make sure each location has a deck of cards.
2. Follow the rest of the steps above. Rather than hand out index cards, you can send bogus e-mails. Otherwise, have the index cards at each location (mailed or prepared ahead of time).
3. You will have to trust each location to keep the index cards secret and to report the true finish times.

CHAPTER 5

Teamwork: Challenges That Require Cooperation

BUTTERMILK LINE

This is . . . An activity in which the participants line themselves up in order of how much they enjoy the taste of buttermilk.

The purpose is . . . For participants to learn about dealing with issues that are not black and white—they have shades of gray.

Use this when . . .
- ➤ The group gets caught up in black-and-white thinking.
- ➤ The group has trouble wrestling with and resolving issues that don't have a clear-cut or easy answer.
- ➤ The group gets caught up in thinking there is only one answer to any situation.

Materials you'll need . . .
- ➤ No materials are necessary for this activity.

Here's how . . .
1. Gather the group in one location with plenty of space to spread out.
2. Tell the group to arrange themselves in one line, single file.
3. Instruct them that the person in the group who loves buttermilk the most should be at one end of the line, and the person who hates it the most should be at the other end of the line.

4. The rest of the participants need to arrange themselves according to their fondness (or not) of
buttermilk in relationship to the two extremes.

Ask these
questions . . .

➤ How did the two end points get filled? *(She said*
she drinks it all the time and loves it; He said he tried
to taste it once and couldn't even get past the smell.)
➤ Which slots were the easiest to fill? Why? *(The two*
extreme points; The people who had actually tasted it
before.)
➤ Which slots were the most difficult to fill? Why?
(The middle points; The people who couldn't remember
what it tasted like; The people who believed it tasted
good just because the boss said it did.)
➤ How did you feel when someone else pressed you
to take a spot in line? *(Like I was being rushed; My*
opinion was being downplayed; I was being helped.)
➤ How did you feel when participants were reluctant
to commit to a place in line? *(Frustrated; They were*
making too big a deal out of this; Anxious that maybe
we were going to run out of time; Not sure why it was
so hard to decide.)
➤ Which situations or decisions back on the job resemble this one?
➤ How can we apply what we learned today to that
situation or decision?

Tips for
success . . .

➤ Once you've described the task, keep quiet. Don't
offer tips or help them get started or get past a
sticking point.
➤ Don't accept a "tie." Remind them that the line is
to be single file, which doesn't allow for ties.
➤ Observe their process; take note of how they resolve questions when things are not clear.
➤ This will be particularly difficult if more than one
participant has never tasted buttermilk (which is

often the case!). Do not offer options for how they can still accomplish the task; let them figure it out.

Try these variations . . .

➤ Have a container of buttermilk on hand and suggest how much the first person versus the last person will be required to drink after the line is formed. (This will increase the anxiety level of some and make the fence sitters more actively involved.)

➤ Buttermilk is a good item, because there are many people who have never tasted it. This causes confusion as to where the group places those people in the line and, more importantly, why. In your environment, another item may work better. If you substitute, use something that will cause the same dilemma as buttermilk.

➤ Increase the stakes by asking the participants to arrange themselves according to how much they love/hate your organization's product or service.

➤ Increase the stakes by asking the participants to arrange themselves according to how much they love/hate your organization's mission statement, vision, goals, values, and so forth.

For virtual teams . . .

This activity works well regardless of the technology used.

1. Have the group make a virtual line by each claiming numbers (1 through however many participants are in the group). Number 1 can be the person who likes buttermilk the most. The highest number is for the person who likes buttermilk the least. No two participants can share a number.

2. All but the first variation listed can work for a virtual team.

CONNECTIONS

This is . . . An activity in which participants join themselves together using their own body parts and/or other items in the room when the participants are called out by the leader.

The purpose is . . . For participants to practice improving their process in a simple game of speed and dexterity. They also get warmed up or energized for a meeting or training.

Use this when . . .
- Participants need help seeing that process improvements are within their grasp.
- You want to warm the participants up physically as well as mentally before a meeting or training.
- You want to add an element of competition to the group.

Materials you'll need . . .
- No materials are necessary for this activity.

Here's how . . .
1. Divide the group into teams of 4–12 participants each.
2. On your signal, the teams are to join together according to the combinations you give them.
3. The first team to make the correct connection wins the round.
4. Have participants disconnect, and then give them the next combination for connecting.
5. After several rounds, declare the team that won the most rounds the ultimate winner.

For example . . .	"Connect using only your thumbs." "Connect using 23 fingers and 1 knee." "Connect using 3 heads, 1 finger, and 1 elbow." "Connect using 5 elbows, 2 knees, and 1 foot." "Connect using 3 thumbs, 3, knees, 3 feet, and 1 table." "Connect using 2 knees, 1 head, 5 hands, and 2 chairs."

Ask these questions . . .

➤ What strategies did you use to be quick? *(We had Bob be the leader, and we all followed his instructions; We stood closer together so we could blend faster.)*

➤ How did your strategies evolve as each round was played? *(We found that assigning certain body parts to people didn't help when those parts weren't used but others were; We learned to use a process for who would contribute what body part.)*

➤ Some of the connections didn't require all the members of your team. How did you feel if you were included or excluded from the connection? *(I felt left out; I didn't care as long as we were fastest; I wanted to be part of all of them.)*

➤ What limited your speed? *(We were too crowded in this corner; We couldn't hear you very well from over here.)*

➤ How could you be even faster?

➤ What implications does this have for us back on the job?

Tips for . . . success

➤ Create lists of connections beforehand—it's difficult to think of different combinations on the spot. Create more than you can imagine using (you'll be surprised at how many you will use!).

➤ Have the teams give a signal when they are done with the connection.

➤ You may want to impose a penalty for groups who call out "done" in *anticipation* of being done in a few seconds (this is very tempting for the highly competitive!).

- Start with easier combinations before challenging the teams with more difficult ones.
- You may want to award a prize to the winning team.
- Depending on your group, you may have to be explicit about touching each other appropriately (e.g., over clothing for knees and elbows).
- Be sensitive to participants with physical disabilities. Find a way to include them fully.

Try these variations . . .

- Play the game with one or more on each team blindfolded.
- Try different sized teams (the larger the team, the more difficult it will be to connect).
- Make the connections more complicated (e.g., 3 ring fingers, 2 index fingers from the 2 youngest people on the team).
- Include more rules (e.g., all body parts must be have a sheet of paper separating them at the contact point).
- Write the connections on a board, and allow only a certain number of participants to see them. These participants must communicate the requirements to the rest of the team.
- Have each team select a leader. Tell the leaders what the connections are. The leaders then coordinate their teams without participating physically.

For virtual teams . . .

This activity works well with virtual teams in which the number of participants at each location is roughly the same.
1. Have the people at each location be one team.
2. Follow the rest of the steps above. You may want a judge at each location. If not, you will have to trust each team to be honest about the true finish time.
3. Be aware that while this activity may pull the participants in each location together, it may also foster their competitiveness with other locations.

CROSSING THE LINE

This is . . .   A paired exercise in which partners try to get each other to cross an imaginary line between them.

The purpose is . . .   For participants to see how readily they create win–lose scenarios when win–win solutions are possible.

Use this when . . .
- ➤ Individuals are not seeking creative solutions to problems.
- ➤ The group is caught up in win–lose thinking.
- ➤ You don't have prep time and/or materials for anything more elaborate.

Materials you'll need . . .   No materials are necessary for this activity.

Here's how . . .
1. Have the participants pair up.
2. Have the paired members stand opposite each other, with about 3–4 feet of space between them.
3. Have them imagine that there is a line drawn on the floor between them and their partner.
4. Tell them that those who get their partner to cross the line will win.
5. Give them 60 seconds to accomplish this.

Ask these questions . . .
- ➤ How many tried to use force? *(Show of hands.)*
- ➤ How many tried to talk the other person into moving first? *(Show of hands.)*

> What were some of the arguments you used? *(I tried to bribe her with some candy back on my desk; I was trying to get him to see that I had a better view out the window from my position.)*
> How many found a win–win solution? *(Show of hands.)*
> Why did you assume that one of you had to win and one lose? *(You said "win," and that conjures up competition and someone having to lose; I didn't think we could both win, just one of us.)*
> For those of you who did, how did you come up with a win–win solution? *(We realized quickly that neither of us was going to move just to let the other one win alone; I wanted both of us to be successful.)*
> Do we create win–lose situations at work without exploring the possibility of finding a win–win solution?
> How can we find more win–win solutions back on the job?

Tips for success . . .
> Don't allow too much time to think or strategize. You want them to react as they naturally do at work with time pressure.
> Make sure there is plenty of room for the pairs to spread out. They don't have to be all lined up.
> Don't clarify or elaborate on the rules or the objective of the game. If they ask, just repeat that they win by getting their partner to cross the line.

Try these variations . . .
> Rather than pairs, have the group divide into teams. Equal-sized teams oppose each other over the imaginary line. Announce that the team that gets everyone from the other team to cross the line will win.
> Teams get 1 point each time one person from the other team crosses over the line; the objective is to

get the most points possible (which would be for all people on all teams to cross the line!).

For virtual teams . . . This activity works well with virtual teams in which there are pairs (or other sized groups) of participants at each location.
1. Participants pair up with someone at their own location.
2. Follow the steps above.

 # DOLLAR BILL

This is . . .	An activity in which pairs of participants question each other about the details of a $1 bill.
The purpose is . . .	For participants to see that familiarity can breed mindlessness about service levels, product quality, or relationship building.
Use this when . . .	➤ Individuals are missing valuable details in their work. ➤ Individuals are cutting corners or glossing over important details that ultimately do have an impact on quality. ➤ Work tasks that are routine or mundane (but important) are being avoided or done poorly.
Materials you'll need . . .	➤ A $1 bill for each pair of participants.
Here's how . . .	1. Have the participants pair up. 2. One partner in each pair takes the $1 bill and looks at the front of the bill while not allowing his or her partner to see it. 3. The bill holder creates and asks the partner seven questions about the details on the face of the bill. 4. Each pair keeps track of how many questions are answered correctly. 5. The other partner then takes the $1 bill and looks at the back of it. Again, the opposite partner is not allowed to see that side of the bill.

6. These bill holders create and ask the partner seven questions about the details on the back of the bill.

7. Each pair again keeps track of how many questions are answered correctly.

For example . . . "How many times is the number 1 spelled out on this side?"

"How many digits are in the serial number on the front?"

"What three words are printed closest to the top of the bill?"

"Where is George Washington looking?"

"Does it say 'Washington' or 'George Washington' under his picture?"

"How many arrows is the eagle clutching in its talon?"

"Which way is the eagle's head turned?"

Even tricky questions are OK: "How many times does it say 'In God We Trust' on the front?" (The answer is zero.)

Ask these questions . . .
- What were your scores?
- Which questions were easier—the ones about the front or the back of the bill? Why? *(The front, because she asked questions about the picture of Washington and I remembered it well; The back was harder because I don't see it as much.)*
- We handle these bills almost daily, so why did we miss so many simple questions about them? *(We don't really pay attention when we use them; We don't notice the details; The questions were too hard.)*
- What details are we missing here on the job?
- What can we gain by paying more attention to details about customers? Processes? Coworkers? Costs?

Tips for success . . .
- Give several examples of questions off the top of your head for each side—just to show them that

creating the questions doesn't have to be stressful. Allow them to use some of your examples.

➤ Encourage participants to ask one or two tricky questions among the more traditional ones. Give an example of a tricky question.

Try these variations . . .

➤ Let both partners handle the bill for 30 seconds before beginning the exercise, but don't tell them why.

➤ If your organization's product lends itself to the activity, use it instead of the $1 bill.

➤ Ask questions about a well-used room or portion of your work environment.

➤ Use a common form from your organization instead of the $1 bill.

➤ Rather than having the partners create the questions, you come with a list of all the questions to be asked. You read the questions. The bill holder checks the accuracy of his or her partner's answers and keeps score.

For virtual teams . . .

This activity works well with virtual teams in which there are pairs (or other sized groups) of participants at each location.

1. Participants pair up with someone at their own location.
2. Make sure each partnership has a $1 bill.
3. Follow the steps above.

HOUSE

This is . . . An activity in which small teams draw a picture of a house—two lines at a time—without speaking to each other.

The purpose is . . . For participants to learn to bend and adjust to others' direction, focus, or influence.

Use this when . . .
- ➤ The group needs practice being creative together.
- ➤ Individuals need to go with the flow more when working with the group.
- ➤ Individuals have trouble adjusting and making the best of what is.

Materials you'll need . . .
- ➤ A pen or marker for each team.
- ➤ A piece of paper for each team (letter size or larger).

Here's how . . .
1. Divide the group into teams of 2–3 participants.
2. Give each team one piece of paper and one pen or marker.
3. Have each team draw a detailed picture of a house, two lines at a time.
4. Each participant will draw two lines, and then pass the pen or marker to the next participant to draw another two lines.
5. Repeat this order until the drawing of the house is completed. The pen may go around the team several times until everyone agrees the drawing is finished.
6. Participants may not talk to anyone while planning or drawing the house.

Ask these questions . . .

➤ How much did you lead or follow? Why? *(She seemed so determined to have it drawn her way; Even though he didn't talk, he was directing us; I wanted to be sure it looked good, and the others didn't seem to care.)*

➤ To what degree did you go with the flow, or how much did you resist? *(I went with the flow because she was pretty determined; I didn't resist, because after all it was just a picture of a house and didn't really matter.)*

➤ What did you find most frustrating about this process? *(That we couldn't talk—I didn't know what they were doing when they made some pretty bizarre lines; She seemed perturbed every time I drew my lines.)*

➤ How did you deal with your frustration? *(I clammed up; I shot angry glances; I just let it go; I sighed loudly; I just gave up.)*

➤ What do you wish your partner(s) had or hadn't done? *(She should have visually checked with us before drawing that second line; He should have engaged more than just drawing random lines that meant nothing.)*

➤ What planning, if any, happened before the first line was drawn?

➤ What implication does this have for us back on the job?

Tips for success . . .

➤ Monitor and help them keep the silence rule (as much fun as they are having, it will be difficult for them to remember not to comment even in a positive, reinforcing way—"ooh, I like that").

➤ Determine before the activity how strict you want to be. For example, is a line only straight? What if someone draws a very long line with curves and corners—basically drawing half the house with one line? Neither way is good or bad; just be clear (or vague) on the rules. You may even leave such questions to the teams to decide. If so, during the Debrief ask how the decisions were made, how the decisions impacted results, and so forth.

➤ As they work, observe what they do that is effective, and bring that out during the Debrief.

➤ Remember: Everyone on the team must continue to add two lines until *everyone* agrees the picture is finished.

Try these variations . . .

➤ Limit the number of lines drawn each time to one, not two.

➤ Draw something other than a house—perhaps a picture of your organization's building, its product, or its logo.

➤ Use toothpicks or pieces of thread or string to "draw" the house.

➤ Use pipe cleaners to build a house rather than draw it.

For virtual teams . . .

This activity works well with virtual teams in which there are pairs (or other sized groups) of participants at each location.

1. Make sure each partnership has the necessary materials

2. Participants pair up with someone at their own location.

3. Follow the steps above.

X, Y, Z, ___ LETTER #27

This is . . . A creative activity in which teams develop a new letter to be added to the end of the alphabet.

The purpose is . . . For participants to learn to be imaginative and creative.

Use this when . . .
- The group lacks creativity.
- The group needs help thinking beyond the typical or common answers.
- You don't have prep time and/or materials for anything more elaborate.

Materials you'll need . . .
- Flip chart and markers (optional).
- Prizes for the winning team (optional).

Here's how . . .
1. Divide the group into teams of 4–6 members.
2. Each team has 10 minutes to create a new letter to add to the alphabet.
3. Each team presents their new letter to the rest of the group—the symbol as well as its pronunciation and examples of its use in common words.
4. The group votes on the best new letter.

Ask these questions . . .
- How did you decide on what letter to develop? *(We looked at sounds we often make that require so many letters to write; We focused more on the symbol and didn't really worry much about the letter's use or sound.)*
- How did you determine its use? *(We polled ourselves on the most common sounds that take more than one letter; We just tossed a coin; She was so determined we just went with what she wanted.)*

- What fostered creativity in your group? What hindered it? *(Listening to each others' ideas before commenting on any of them; Encouraging each other to be more and more outrageous; Judging each of the ideas as it was thrown out quickly stifled the idea flow.)*
- How can we apply this creative thinking back on the job?

Tips for success . . .
- Encourage participants not to use letters or other symbols borrowed from other languages. Create something completely new.
- Don't let individuals vote for the letter that their team developed (otherwise you risk everyone on a team voting for their own letter and no one winning).
- Don't help the groups by offering ideas for types of letters to create. Let them struggle with the challenge and find a creative solution. If it's nowhere near where you were thinking, appreciate their out-of-the-box thinking and creativity!

Try these variations . . .
- Challenge the teams to also show where the new letter would fit on a standard keyboard.
- Have the group create a new word to be included in the dictionary. Encourage them to create a word that doesn't exist but would be particularly helpful in your organization or your industry.

For virtual teams . . .
This activity works well with virtual teams in which the number of participants at each location is roughly the same.
1. Make sure each location has a set of materials.
2. Follow the rest of the steps above.
3. Be aware that while this activity may pull the participants in each location together, it may also foster their competitiveness with other locations.

LICENSE PLATES

This is . . .   An activity in which teams (or individuals) create slogans from letters in the format of a vanity license plate.

The purpose is . . .   For participants to learn to be creative while focusing on what's important to them about their work or a specific project or initiative.

Use this when . . .
➤ Individuals are not thinking as creatively as they should.
➤ The group needs a boost of energy.
➤ The group is not really together with their thinking or motivation.

Materials you'll need . . .
➤ Prepared "license plates." Create them by writing (or printing) six to eight random letters (you may include a digit or two) horizontally on a page to resemble a typical license plate. You may use the same license plate for all teams or make a different one for each team.

Here's how . . .
1. Divide the group into teams of 3–5 participants.
2. Give each team a "license plate."
3. Teams have 8 minutes to create a team-related slogan.
4. Teams use the letters from their license plates as the first letters of each word of the slogans or as part of a word.
5. Have teams share their slogans with the rest of the group.

For example . . .	RSBPPL = ReSponsiBility [needs] Practice and Patience and Love. HBGLTR = Having Big Goals [makes us] Leverage Team Resources. WODNMSS = Working Overtime Doesn't Necessarily Mean Sure Success; When Older Data Need a Makeover, Send in the Specialists.
Ask these questions . . .	➤ How did you agree on the words you would use? *(We threw out a bunch of options and then played with each one; She came up with something close to a finished tag line right off the bat, so we just tweaked it.)* ➤ Did you allow yourselves to put words in between letters (words like "a," "the," "in") or were you strictly adhering to the letters? Why? *(We stuck with letter for letter, but now that I see some of the other groups, I wonder why we felt so bound; We didn't let the letters confine us; We used only the letters given, because we didn't want to make it any easier for ourselves.)* ➤ What words didn't you use? Why not? *(We thought of a few variations that were funny but probably inappropriate in the workplace; We stayed away from negative connotations; We didn't want to use people's names.)* ➤ How collaborative was your effort? *(Very, we couldn't have done it without everyone's input; Some of us weren't very creative, so we waited till others threw out a few options, then we were good at helping adjust them for a finished line.)* ➤ How can we apply how we worked together here back on the job?
Tips for success . . .	➤ Be prepared to show an example or two, so the group understands the concept.

> Have teams assign a spokesperson to deliver the final slogan.

> Offer extra credit for humor!

Try these variations . . .

> As an introductory icebreaker, have each individual use a license plate to create a slogan that describes himself or herself.

> Have a pre-team-building activity. Ask each team to create a license plate for another team. Participants can use challenging letters or combinations of letters. Then, have teams trade the license plates with each other and begin the activity above.

> Use the same license plate for all teams. After sharing the results, have the teams vote on the best one (team members cannot vote for their own slogan). Award a prize to the winners.

> Specify the theme for the slogans—project purpose, commitment to customer, quality, teamwork.

> Play several quick rounds. Have the teams keep their license plate and come up with several different slogans based on different topics you give them.

> Make the activity easier by allowing the teams to change ONE letter on their license plate to accommodate their preferred slogan.

> No time to prepare license plates? Make one up on the spot and post it so everyone can see.

For virtual teams . . .

This activity works well with virtual teams in which the number of participants at each location is roughly the same.

1. Make sure each location has materials.
2. Follow the rest of the steps above.
3. Be aware that while this activity may pull the participants in each location together, it may also foster their competitiveness with other locations.

ONE SYLLABLE

This is . . .   A game in which teams compete to guess hidden words by hearing clues composed entirely of one-syllable words.

The purpose is . . .   For participants to become more aware of their communication patterns and to practice their focus on details.

Use this when . . .
- The group needs to learn to approach simple problems more creatively and/or spontaneously.
- The group is overlooking important details.
- Individuals are reckless, or not being careful, in their communication.

Materials you'll need . . .
- Index cards, each with a common place, person, or thing written on it that will be guessed by the teams.
- A stopwatch or other timekeeper.

Here's how . . .
1. Divide the group into two teams of roughly equal size.
2. Team A chooses one member to be the Clue Giver.
3. Start the timer when Team A's Clue Giver draws the first card.
4. The Clue Giver gives clues to Team A so they can guess what's written on the card. The Clue Giver must use words that have only one syllable in them.
5. Team A tries to guess what's on the card. Guesses can be made simultaneously and often. There is no penalty for wrong answers.

6. For each correct answer, Team A gets 1point.
7. The Clue Giver can pass on any card he or she desires. No points are awarded (or deducted) for a passed card.
8. Team B listens to Team A's Clue Giver and calls out if they hear him or her use any word that has more than one syllable.
9. If the Clue Giver is caught using multisyllable words, the card is returned and no point is given.
10. After 1 minute, call "time" and tally Team A's points.
11. Repeat the process for Team B.

For example . . .

"This was the first man to lead our states when they first came like one . . . (George Washington)"
"This is what you eat when you need a sweet. It's brown and tastes so good. You can break it or let it melt in your mouth. It's best with . . . (chocolate)"
"This is a large city in the . . . (NO! *city* has two syllables)"

Ask these questions . . .

➤ What was the key to your success as the Clue Giver? *(Slowing down my speaking; Using lots of gestures; Passing difficult cards and doing only the ones I was confident about.)*
➤ What was the most difficult part as you listened for multisyllable words? *(I got too wound up trying to guess the right answer myself; Some words are common, I didn't hear them as having more than one syllable.)*
➤ How did it feel when you were caught using multisyllable words or when your team's Clue Giver was caught? *(Frustrated; Angry; They were being particularly picky even after we had let them get a few by.)*
➤ How does this exercise relate to our work or our organization?
➤ What can we learn from this that we can apply back on the job?

Tips for	➤ Err on the side of too many cards rather than not
success . . .	enough. Remember, Clue Givers can pass on any
	card, so they might run through the stack pretty
	quickly.

Tips for success . . .

➤ Err on the side of too many cards rather than not enough. Remember, Clue Givers can pass on any card, so they might run through the stack pretty quickly.

➤ Declare up front whether gestures and/or sound effects are allowed as part of the clues.

➤ Have the Clue Giver discard into two piles—one pile holds cards his or her team guessed correctly, and the other pile holds passed cards or cards for which the Clue Giver was caught using multi-syllable words. One stack represents the number of points earned, and the other stack can be reused.

➤ If you run out of clue cards, have the teams create more. The cards Team A creates are used by Team B and vise versa.

Try these variations . . .

➤ Have the teams create the cards for each other (Team A prepares a stack of cards that the Clue Giver on Team B will use for his or her team and vice versa).

➤ Play several rounds. For each round, the teams must use a different Clue Giver.

➤ Do not allow Clue Givers to pass on a difficult card.

➤ Deduct 1 point for each card that is passed.

➤ Deduct 2 points for each card that is passed.

➤ Deduct 1 point when a multisyllable word is used.

For virtual teams . . .

This activity works well regardless of the technology used.

1. Make sure each location has plenty of cards for play.
2. Follow the steps above.
3. If audio is not available, participants can type in their clues and their guesses.
4. All but the first variation listed can work for a virtual team.

PUZZLED VISION

This is . . .   A competitive activity in which participants put together a puzzle, sometimes while seeing what the final picture should look like and sometimes not.

The purpose   For participants to understand the value of sharing a
is . . .   common vision and working toward it.

Use this   ➤ A new team is forming.
when . . .   ➤ A significant project is beginning.
    ➤ Individuals need to bond together and to better focus their work efforts.
    ➤ The vision is new or changing.

Materials   ➤ A puzzle for each team.
you'll need . . .   ➤ The puzzle boxes or pictures of what the completed puzzles should look like.
    ➤ A prize for the winning team (optional).

Here's   1. Divide the group into teams of 2–6 participants.
how . . .   2. Give each team all the pieces of one puzzle.
    3. Have team members place their pieces face up on the table (none interlocked!) and in no particular order or pattern.
    4. Before the teams begin moving the pieces around, ask them to guess what their completed puzzle picture will look like.
    5. If they get a general idea (e.g., a pony) ask for details about the picture ("What do you think the pony is doing?").

6. Do not confirm or deny their guesses, just note what they guessed.
7. Give half the teams a picture of their puzzle. The other half of the teams shouldn't see the pictures of their puzzles.
8. Ask all the teams to build their puzzles as quickly as possible.
9. Award a prize to the winning (fastest) team (optional).

Ask these questions . . .

➤ Which teams finished first? Why is that?

➤ How did having the picture help? *(It was easier to divide the work when we had a master plan; It helped us stay focused; It guided us when we were stuck.)*

➤ What troubles did you have without the picture? *(We didn't know what we were doing; We got distracted and frustrated.)*

➤ How is having the picture for the puzzle construction similar to having a shared vision for our organization? *(A vision helps us stay focused; We all bring a little piece to the grand vision; The vision can't happen by the efforts of just one or two.)*

➤ What if someone had puzzle pieces that didn't belong to the puzzle? *(Perhaps he doesn't fit with the vision and should go somewhere else where the vision speaks to his personal goals; Maybe he just needs help understanding the vision, so he can bring the right things to the table.)*

➤ What is OUR shared vision?

➤ How can we use this vision to help us be more successful?

Tips for success . . .

➤ Puzzles should be identical or at least have the same number of pieces and the same degree of difficulty.

> Make sure the puzzles have enough pieces that the final picture is not easily determined by a few pieces held together, or the activity will lose its punch. If the teams will have fewer members (3–5), use puzzles that have 25–50 pieces. Larger teams are best with 100-piece puzzles.

Try these variations . . .

> For groups so small that only one team of 2–6 exists: Run the activity twice, and time the results for comparison. First run it without letting the participants see the puzzle box. The second time, use a different but similar-sized puzzle, and let participants see the box.
> Try using children's puzzles that include a frame. What does the frame represent (legal parameters, limits to an otherwise broader vision)?

For virtual teams . . .

This activity isn't suitable for virtual teams.

REACH FOR THE STARS

This is . . .   A quick exercise in which participants reach as high as they can and then reach even higher.

The purpose is . . .   For participants to learn that when they really give it their all, they can usually accomplish more than they originally thought possible.

Use this when . . .
- ➤ Goals seem lofty or out of reach.
- ➤ Individuals need to get pumped up or excited at the beginning of a project or initiative.
- ➤ You don't have prep time and/or materials for anything more elaborate.

Materials you'll need . . .   No materials are necessary for this activity.

Here's how . . .
1. Have all the participants stand up.
2. Have all the participants reach upward as far as they can. Have them try to touch the ceiling.
3. Pause for a moment for them to see how high they are reaching.
4. Then challenge them to try harder; see if they can reach even higher!

Ask these questions . . .
- ➤ How high did you reach the first time? The second time? *(The first time I thought I was reaching pretty high, but the second time I did get higher; I couldn't*

get any higher the second time, maybe just a quarter inch.)

➤ Why were you able to reach higher the second time, even though you were reaching "as high as you can" the first time? *(I guess because you challenged us to; Maybe I held back a little the first time because there was no real reason to give it my all yet.)*

➤ How does this exercise compare with our efforts back on the job?

Tips for success . . .

➤ Be sure to use the words "as high as you can" (or even "as high as you possibly can") on the first round. The second round is much more powerful when you can compare the first "as high as you can" with the second "as high as you can!"

➤ During the Debrief, help participants come to realize (without you having to state it) that often our first effort is rarely our best or that, when challenged, we can often do better than we originally thought.

Try these variations . . .

➤ For a very athletic group, time them running a distance rather than reaching.

➤ Use another, more challenging task (putting a random deck of cards in order, stacking a pile of blocks, alphabetizing a set of words).

For virtual teams . . .

This activity works well regardless of the technology used.

STICK IN THE MIDDLE

This is . . . An activity in which partners lead each other around the room holding a stick physically between their bodies.

The purpose is . . . Participants learn that both Leaders and Followers have a responsibility to each other for the success of any endeavor.

Use this when . . .
- Individuals don't see their own role in making their Leader successful.
- The group is expecting too much from the Leader.
- The group needs a physical activity to get the energy up.

Materials you'll need . . .
- Enough wooden dowels (3–4 feet in length) for each pair of participants.

Here's how . . .
1. Have the participants pair up.
2. Have them place the dowel between their stomachs (end to end).
3. Instruct one partner to lead the other one around the room for 3–4 minutes (stop them sooner if the energy level gets low).
4. Have them switch roles—the other partner now leads—for 3–4 minutes.

Ask these questions . . .
- How much pressure did you use when you were leading? Following?

- ➤ Was the pressure different leading versus following? Why?
- ➤ For those of you who dropped the dowel, what do you think caused it? *(She wasn't pushing back enough; He tried to back up without warning me first; I wasn't paying attention when he turned.)*
- ➤ What responsibility did the Leader have for the success of the walk around? *(She had to watch and gauge how the Follower was responding; He had to explain beforehand where she was going.)*
- ➤ What responsibility did the Follower have for the success of the walk around? *(He had to anticipate the Leader's moves; She had to question and challenge the Leader's assumptions.)*
- ➤ Are we all Leaders even if we don't have anyone reporting to us on the organization chart? *(Yes; No; It depends.)*
- ➤ How does what we experienced here relate to you as a Leader and/or Follower back on the job?

Tips for success . . .

- ➤ If you are concerned about participants hurting themselves with the wooden dowel, cut the same length from the foam "noodles" commonly used in swimming pools or use cardboard tubes from rolls of paper towels (you may have to tape two or more end to end to get the right length).
- ➤ Don't let the participants touch each other (no holding hands or hands on shoulders to help guide).
- ➤ Encourage participants to not rest the dowel on a belt buckle or other accessory that would make the exercise too easy.
- ➤ Have a longer dowel prepared if any participants are in wheelchairs or have other special needs.
- ➤ Ease the pressure of the dowel ends by wrapping them with a towel. Alternatively, cut holes in tennis balls and stick the balls on the ends.

Try these   ➤ Blindfold one or both partners for the exercise.
variations . . . ➤ Make a rule of no talking for one or both partners.
                     ➤ Prohibit the Follower from asking questions or
                       challenging the Leader. He or she may only say
                       "Yes, Boss" when given direction.
                     ➤ Lay out a path that each pair should follow, with
                       some obstacles, if desired (make sure the paths and
                       obstacles are safe).
                     ➤ Have pairs race each other from one point to
                       another.

For virtual This activity works well with virtual teams in which
teams . . . there are at least pairs of participants at each location.
                 1. Make sure you have enough wooden dowels at
                    each location.
                 2. Participants pair up with someone at their own
                    location.
                 3. Follow the steps above.

CHAPTER 6

Creativity: Challenges That Encourage Out-of-the-Box Thinking

 **ABCS**

This is . . . A game in which participants build letters of the alphabet with odds and ends found around the workplace.

The purpose is . . . For participants to learn to solve problems creatively using mundane objects.

Use this when . . .
- ➤ Creative thinking is not happening enough.
- ➤ The group members are not cooperating with each other as well as they should.
- ➤ The group needs a shot of competitiveness to energize it.

Materials you'll need . . .
- ➤ Two identical sets of common items found around the office, one for each team, packed in a bag or a box.

Here's how . . .
1. Divide the group into teams of 3–5 participants.
2. Give each team a bag of items commonly found around the office.
3. Teams are to use these items to construct the entire alphabet (or as much as they can) in 10 minutes.
4. The alphabet must be constructed in order (no jumping ahead to easy letters like "I" and "X").
5. The winning team is the one that gets furthest in the alphabet.

For example . . . A good set of items might be five paper clips, five drinking straws or coffee stirrers, five staples, five pencils, five rubber bands, five sticky notes, five thumbtacks, five sticks of gum, and one sheet of paper.

Ask these questions . . .
➤ How did you get as far as you did? *(We divided ourselves into planning and building subteams; We decided to use the straight items quickly for straight letters like A.)*
➤ What would have made it easier to get further? *(More time; We should have planned ahead instead of just going from one letter to the next; Not worry too much about the letters being perfectly formed; Not having to do the letters in order.)*
➤ How did you feel when I called out "one more minute?" *(I felt rushed; I wondered how we compared with the other teams; I was relieved it was almost over.)*
➤ What did you learn with this activity that can be applied back on the job?

Tips for success . . .
➤ Teams rarely have enough time to finish this task; expect this and discuss afterward.
➤ For highly competitive teams, give a warning when the time is about to end (this heightens the pressure).
➤ Make sure there are enough items in the bag to get through several letters. For example, it would be impossible to do more than a few letters with only three paperclips and three toothpicks. Teams will immediately realize this and get discouraged.
➤ Declare up front whether they are allowed to rip paper, break pencils, and so forth.

Try these variations . . .
➤ Don't allow any talking during the building time.
➤ Allow participants to use only one of their hands during the building time.

- Shorten the time, and, instead of building the alphabet, have the teams build letters to spell your organization's name or a series of numbers.
- Do not provide the materials. Explain the activity, and then give the teams 3–5 minutes to find the materials they will use. Limit the number of similar items ("No more than seven of any one item."). Deduct one letter from their score for every 10 seconds late they are getting back to the room.

For virtual teams . . .   This activity isn't suitable for virtual teams.

FAILURE STRATEGIES

This is . . .   A creative brain-storming activity in which participants think negatively to get a positive outcome.

The purpose is . . .   For participants to find new solutions to old
problems by thinking differently about them.

Use this when . . .
- ➤ The group has an important goal or project that simply must go well.
- ➤ The group is overly confident in its ability and need a reality check.
- ➤ Creative problem solving is not happening often enough.

Materials you'll need . . .
- ➤ No materials are necessary for this activity.

Here's how . . .
1. Divide the group into teams of 3–6 members.
2. Present all the teams with the same organizational goal or project plan.
3. Give the teams 5 minutes to come up with the three to five best ways to ensure that the goal or project *fails*.
4. Have the teams report on their sure-fire failure strategies.

For example . . .   "We think this could fail miserably if we did the
following three things:

> ➤ Minimize Tony's input and involvement.
> ➤ Not communicate with our sister organizations.
> ➤ Have only people who agree with us on the team."

Ask these questions . . .
➤ How easy or hard was it to come up with failure strategies? *(It was easy, just be pessimistic; It was harder than we thought; Harder on the parts that we personally built into the plan.)*
➤ How did you come up with your strategies? *(We looked for weak links in the logic; We looked for places we thought were iffy; We each identified one problem we saw and then prioritized; We put ourselves in the place of our customers looking at this.)*
➤ What value do these failure strategies have for us now? *(They help us see some holes in our planning; We can anticipate where we really need to be careful; We can plan for problems before they take us by surprise.)*
➤ How should we use our failure strategies to strengthen our plan or goal now?

Tips for success . . .
➤ Don't help the teams. If they struggle for a minute or two, let them. If you help them, they will follow your lead instead of their own initiatives.
➤ Be careful to not let the session turn into a gripe session or a hand-wringing worry session in which the group starts to convince itself all is lost!
➤ Point out that this is one of the ways team members who tend to play "devil's advocate" actually do contribute to a team's success. Help them learn to leverage these contributions positively rather than to write the members off as "nay sayers."

Try these variations . . .
➤ Give each team a different part of the project plan to find failure strategies for.

➤ Add a second round. Have the teams swap their lists of failure strategies. Then have each team make these failures even stronger before discussing resolutions.

➤ Rather than *strategies* for ensuring failure, have the groups determine the best *reasons* to *allow* the project to fail. This will lead to discussions about motivation and energy toward the success of a particular effort.

For virtual teams . . .   This activity works well with virtual teams in which the number of participants at each location is roughly the same.

1. Participants at each location become a team.
2. Follow Steps 2–4 as outlined.

FISHBOWL

This is . . . A think-outside-of-the-box activity in which participants create a fishbowl out of puzzle pieces that were
not designed to make a fishbowl.

The purpose For participants to think outside the box and use
is . . . creativity to solve a problem together.

Use this ➤ Creative problem solving is lacking.
when . . . ➤ Individuals are not cooperating as well as they
should.
➤ The group needs to loosen up and have a little fun
as the members work together.

Materials ➤ One to two jigsaw puzzles per team.
you'll need . . .

Here's 1. Divide the group into teams of 3–6 members.
how . . . 2. Give each team the pieces from one to two
puzzles.
3. Allow the teams 10 minutes to create a fishbowl
using only the puzzle pieces in front of them.
4. After 10 minutes, look at each other's fishbowls
and discuss.

Ask these ➤ How did you solve the challenge? *(We stacked the*
questions . . . *pieces to build a 3-D fishbowl; We used the pieces to*
draw an outline of a fishbowl and then used these
other pieces to represent fish.)
➤ What other ideas did you consider? *(We considered*
interlocking the pieces in a 3-D model; We almost used

the back side of the pieces for a more neutral color
background on which to create them.)

➤ How did you agree on the approach? *(We voted;*
We just went with the loudest person; We only had
one idea.)

➤ How difficult was it for you to stop viewing the
puzzle pieces in the customary way (things that
should be interlocked to make a predetermined
picture)?

➤ Where do we have similar, limiting "puzzle pieces"
at work that we could be looking at more creatively?

Tips for
success . . .

➤ Use puzzles that have enough pieces that it is not
easy to determine what is on each individual piece
(puzzles with 100–500 pieces work best).

➤ Make sure none of the puzzles has fish, fishbowls,
or similar themes in them. The challenge is to
make a fishbowl, not solve the puzzle in the customary way.

➤ Try not to give the teams ideas on how to accomplish their task; this can stifle or limit their own
creativity. If they ask if the puzzle pieces are supposed to make a picture of a fishbowl, just repeat
the original instruction, "Create a fishbowl using
only those puzzle pieces."

Try these
variations . . .

➤ Allow the teams to use other props available in the
room.

➤ Change the fishbowl to something relevant to
your business (e.g., have teachers create a school,
an apple, or a text book).

➤ Use interlocking building blocks instead of puzzle
pieces, but stipulate that no block can be locked to
another block in the final solution.

For virtual
teams . . .

This activity isn't suitable for virtual teams.

 **FIST**

This is . . .	A paired exercise in which one participant is challenged with opening the fist of his or her partner.
The purpose is . . .	For participants to learn that not every interaction needs to be confrontational and not every confrontation needs to be a battle.
Use this when . . .	➤ Individuals are making problems more difficult or more complicated than they need to be.
	➤ The group is seeing force as the only way to resolve differences.
	➤ You don't have prep time and/or materials for anything more elaborate.
Materials you'll need . . .	➤ No materials are necessary for this activity.
Here's how . . .	1. Have the participants pair up.
	2. Each pair designates who is A and who is B.
	3. Participant A makes a fist and presents it to Participant B.
	4. Participant Bs have exactly 30 seconds to open their partner's fist.
Ask these questions . . .	➤ How many tried to physically force the fist open? *(Show of hands.)*
	➤ How many tried to bribe your partner? *(Show of hands.)*

- How many tried tickling your partner? *(Show of hands.)*
- How many tried to manipulate your partner? *(Show of hands.)*
- How many merely asked your partner to open his or her fist? *(Show of hands.)*
- Why did some of you make this more difficult than it had to be? *(I thought it was a contest; It couldn't be as easy as it sounded on the surface; I knew she wouldn't cooperate if I just asked her.)*
- Why did you resort to force? *(When you said "open their fist" I thought that meant I had to be the one to open it, so I used force; I assumed you set it up so that he was supposed to try to resist my efforts; The fist itself looked threatening.)*
- Was your reaction here similar to how you approach challenges back on the job?
- What did we learn here today that we can apply to problem solving back on the job?

Tips for success . . .

- Don't spend a lot of time setting this activity up. Don't give them time to strategize. Set it up quickly and then start the time ticking immediately. This is not a lesson in planning; you want them to react as they typically would.
- Don't allow more than 60 seconds for the activity. The short time frame encourages participants to react without much thinking.

Try these variations . . .

- Make the setup look even more like a contest by blindfolding one of the partners.
- Have only a few partnerships do this activity. Send all who will participate out of the room and bring them back in two at a time. The rest of the group observes each partnership struggle with the

activity and debriefs after all the pairs have taken a turn.

➤ Instead of making a fist, have each Participant A hold a penny. Participant B has 30 seconds to get the penny from A. How many used force? How many merely asked?

For virtual teams . . . This activity works well with virtual teams in which there are at least pairs of participants at each location.

1. Participants pair up with someone at their own location.
2. Follow the steps above.

JOB TITLES

This is . . . An activity in which participants give themselves new job titles that better reflect the impact they would like to have at work.

The purpose is . . . For participants to link their behavior and performance with impact and end results.

Use this when . . .
➤ Individuals are stuck in policies, procedures, and bureaucracies.
➤ Individuals are not focusing on their own impact or final results.
➤ You don't have prep time and/or materials for anything more elaborate.

Materials you'll need . . .
➤ No materials are necessary for this activity.

Here's how . . .
1. Participants think of a new job title for themselves that is NOT related to tasks or responsibility but rather focuses on the impact they wish to have at work.
2. Participants share their new job titles with the rest of the group. Do not let anyone comment, critique, or otherwise give feedback on the new titles.
3. Next, challenge the participants to change the title and make it even better—add an exciting adjective, change a word to make it more powerful, or scratch it and think of a new one.

4. Share the new and improved job titles with the rest of the group.
5. Encourage participants to LIVE that job title for the rest of the meeting.
6. Conduct the Debrief at the end of the meeting, after everyone has lived his or her new job title for a while.

For example . . . "My regular job title is *Customer Service Rep.* My new one is *Customer Caregiver* because I want to emphasize the impact I want to have on our customers. I want them to feel that we care."

"Now I've changed my job title from *Customer Caregiver* to *Caregiver to Our Business Partners.* Because of the unique nature of our business, our customers really are more than just customers, right? We should keep that in mind as we deal with them, as we care for them."

Ask these questions . . .
➤ How difficult was it to think of a new title with this different slant? *(It was easier than I thought once I focused on the results I want to achieve; Harder than it sounded; Tough because my title already pretty much says it all.)*
➤ How did you feel or react when I asked you to improve the great title you had come up with? *(Are you kidding, this already is a great new title; I figured it could probably be improved a little; I was glad you let us scrap the whole thing because I didn't really like my first attempt.)*
➤ How difficult was it to live the new job title? *(Not at all, it's how I normally do my job anyway; It made it easier to stay focused on what's really important; Difficult until I realized this wasn't a role play, but a chance to redirect my focus.)*

	➤ How can we take what we learned from this exercise and apply it on the job for longer term impact?

Tips for success . . .
➤ Help participants by having a few examples for your own job ready to share. Don't offer suggestions or examples for their jobs, as they may get locked on those and find it more difficult to be creative themselves.

➤ If the new job titles really help, consider changing job titles permanently.

Try these variations . . .
➤ Have the participants think of titles for a role they play in a meeting rather than their full-time job (e.g., Collaborator, Idea Synthesizer, Great Listener). Titles that emphasize the impact they'd like to have in the meeting may be easier to live for the rest of that meeting.

➤ Have participants live their new job titles for a day or a whole week. Debrief after they've had a longer time to experience their "new" selves.

➤ Break into smaller teams, and have each team together think of a new job title for each of its members. The discussion will be very enlightening for you and for them!

For virtual teams . . .
This activity works well regardless of the technology used.

MONSTERS

This is . . .	A creative activity in which participants use art supplies to make monsters that represent current threats and risks that the organization faces.
The purpose is . . .	For participants to become clear about threats and risks in their work or on a project so that they can address them more directly.
Use this when . . .	➤ A project or an initiative is starting up. ➤ A group is feeling overwhelmed with adversity or opposition to their efforts. ➤ Individuals are feeling they are victims.
Materials you'll need . . .	➤ Construction paper, scissors, tape, markers, pipe cleaners, feathers, clay, and arts and craft supplies.
Here's how . . .	1. Divide the group into teams of 3–5 members. 2. Distribute the supplies to each team. 3. Give the teams 10 minutes to make a monster that represents the threats or risks they face as they take on a new project or work on a particular issue. 4. Have the teams share their monsters with the rest of the group.
Ask these questions . . .	➤ What is the value of clarifying who or what our monsters are? *(Sometimes just naming them makes them less formidable; Fear begets fear, and this helps us put things in perspective.)* ➤ Why did you include specific elements in your monster? *(This had to be there to represent the outside pressure we feel; We couldn't use that because we didn't want to hurt someone's feelings.)*

➤ Which threats or risks do you feel are the most important ones to address? *(This one, it's in everyone's monster; That one because it's so all-consuming.)*
➤ How real are these threats and risks? How likely are they to pose a real problem for us?
➤ Do you think the people who represent these threats and risks realize that we see them as such? Should we tell them?
➤ How can we deal most effectively with these threats and risks?

Tips for success . . .
➤ Refrain from commenting on their work until they present the finished product (or you risk inadvertently influencing their work).
➤ Help them see that threats and risks are not necessarily going to trip them up. They actually have two courses of action—one, work to *avoid* the threat or risk, and two, work to *minimize* it's effect if it can't be prevented.

Try these variations . . .
➤ Distribute the supplies to the teams in a way that forces them to barter or share supplies. For example, one team gets all the scissors, one team gets all the pipe cleaners, and so forth.
➤ Limit the amount of supplies available so that scarcity is part of the exercise.
➤ Round 2 of the activity could be to create a bigger, better monster that is capable of devouring (or otherwise neutralizing) the first monster. What kinds of solutions might the bigger GOOD monster represent?

For virtual teams . . .
This activity works well with teams that can see each other and in which the number of participants at each location is roughly the same.
1. Make sure each location has a set of materials.
2. Follow the steps above.

NEWSPAPER COSTUMES

This is . . .	An activity in which teams create costumes for one of their members using only newspaper and tape.
The purpose is . . .	For participants to have some fun while being creative.
Use this when . . .	➤ Individuals need to approach issues more creatively. ➤ The group needs to focus on planning and implementation skills. ➤ The group needs to lighten up and have some fun.
Materials you'll need . . .	➤ One to two newspapers for each team ➤ A roll of tape for each team
Here's how . . .	1. Divide the group into teams of 4–6 members each. 2. Give the teams 10 minutes to create a costume for one of its members entirely out of newspaper and tape.
Ask these questions . . .	➤ How did you decide on what costume to make? *(We each presented one idea and then voted; He had such a great idea to begin with, that's all it took; We agreed it had to have something to do with our organization.)* ➤ What was your strategy for making the costume? *(We divided the labor; She did the tape, I did the fold-*

ing; We all just pitched in and followed his lead; I don't think we had a strategy.)

➤ How creative were you? Now that you see the other costumes, how much more creative could you have been? *(We were pretty creative; We went with what we figured would be "safe"; Now I see we could have been much more inventive with our ideas.)*

➤ What limits our creativity on the job?

➤ How can we be more creative on the job?

Tips for success . . .

➤ Don't offer any ideas; let the teams come up with their own.

➤ If possible, put the teams in separate rooms or place visual barriers between them so they don't see each other's work until the very end.

➤ Be sure each newspaper is about the same size (so one team doesn't complain about getting a small paper while another one gets the large Sunday edition).

Try these variations . . .

➤ Have a costume competition at the end. Each person gets one vote, and no one is allowed to vote for the costume his or her team created. Award a prize to the team that designed the winning costume.

➤ Limit the costumes to a specific category (e.g., typical customers of ours, cartoon characters, famous people) to make it more difficult or to make it fit the theme of a meeting, conference, or retreat.

➤ Instead of tape, use straight pins.

➤ Limit the use of tape by giving each team a certain length (e.g., 12 inches).

➤ Add another item (e.g., a feather, a paper cup, the product your organization produces) that must be incorporated into the costume.

➤ Add a lesson on changing team membership by asking one person from each team to join a different team about 4 minutes into the exercise. During the Debrief, ask questions about how this new team member was welcomed and integrated once he or she arrived, how losing a team member affected the productivity of the group midstream, and so on.

➤ Don't provide newspapers or other supplies. Have the teams go on a mini scavenger hunt—to other departments—to find props they could use to make a costume (newspapers or otherwise).

For virtual teams . . . This activity works well with teams that can see each other and in which the number of participants at each location is roughly the same.

1. Make sure each location has a set of materials.
2. Follow the steps above. Decide whether the costuming must be done on camera (so that the teams can watch each other's progress) or not.
3. Be aware that while this activity may pull the participants in each location together, it may also foster their competitiveness with other locations.

SECRET AGENDA

This is . . . An activity in which participants tell a story together using bizarre words that no one else knows about.

The purpose is . . . For participants to learn to be creative in their thinking

Use this when . . .
> Individuals seem to have their own agenda that is overriding the team agenda.
> Quick, on-your-feet creativity is required but not happening.
> Individuals are not cooperating very well.

Materials you'll need . . .
> A pen and an index card for each participant.

Here's how . . .
1. Give each participant a pen and an index card.
2. Have participants think of a random, bizarre word or phrase and write it on the card. Do not let them tell each other what they wrote; it's a secret.
3. Have them keep the cards hidden so that no one can see them.
4. Say "Once upon a time . . ." and hand the story over to the first participant.
5. The participant adds one to two sentences to the story during which time the participant must use the word(s) he or she wrote on the card.
6. The next participant adds one to two more sentences, again using the word(s) he or she wrote on the card.
7. The story moves around the team until the last person ends it.

For example . . .	Once upon a time . . .
	A man went into a diner and ordered *chopped liver and fish heads* . . .
	The girl sitting next to him asked if her *Raggedy Ann* doll could have a taste . . .
	He said, Sure, but it may not taste all that great. The best fish heads come from *Timbuktu* . . .

Ask these questions . . .

➤ How many of you felt the person before you didn't set you up very well? *(Show of hands.)*

➤ How did that make you feel? *(Frustrated; Annoyed; Challenged.)*

➤ How difficult or easy was it to work your word in when it was time? *(It was hard because the story had nothing to do with my word, and I couldn't figure out how to force it in; It was tough because I felt my word would change the course of the story, and it was going so well up till then.)*

➤ How jarring was it when a word was used that didn't fit the story? *(It felt so forced; It stopped the flow of everything; It felt self-serving and didn't help the story at all.)*

➤ How often do we find ourselves (or others) pushing a secret agenda at work—forcing something in that doesn't fit?

➤ What implication does this have for us back on the job when we encounter obvious secret agendas?

Tips for success . . .

➤ When you ask them to write bizarre words or phrases on their cards, don't tell them what will happen or how the words will be used.

➤ Encourage the story to move quickly. Don't labor over a great story line, or it gets tedious and people will lose interest.

➤ Encourage participants to speak loudly and clearly.

Try these	➤ Have participants swap cards before they start the
variations . . .	story. Now they are forcing words into the story
	that someone else gave them. It may be even more
	difficult. The writer of the card will get an extra
	charge when he or she hears his or her bizarre
	word(s) used by someone else.

➤ Have participants swap cards before they start the story. Now they are forcing words into the story that someone else gave them. It may be even more difficult. The writer of the card will get an extra charge when he or she hears his or her bizarre word(s) used by someone else.

➤ Make it even more challenging. After each participant adds his or her lines, have the group guess which of the word(s) used was on the index card. This will force the speaker to add even more bizarre words to the story to cover up the one he or she has chosen.

➤ Limit the words and phrases on the cards to things related to your organization.

➤ Make the story go around the circle twice. Only once must the card be used; the other time participants can say anything. Can participants guess which times the cards were used?

For virtual teams . . .

This activity works well regardless of the technology used.

1. Make sure each location has a set of materials.
2. All but the first variation listed can work for a virtual team.

STATUE MAKER

This is . . . An activity in which participants use their creativity to create a statue using themselves as the medium.

The purpose is . . . For participants to learn how originality and creativity can be enhanced but that they can also be stifled by too much input.

Use this when . . .
- ➤ Participants are not being as original or creative as they should.
- ➤ The group is overly confident in its creativity.
- ➤ You don't have prep time and/or materials for anything more elaborate.

Materials you'll need . . .
- ➤ No materials are necessary for this activity.

Here's how . . .
1. Take everyone out of the room and line them up.
2. The first three people in line come into the room.
3. Tell them to pose and become a human statue of three people playing football.
4. When they are in position, invite the next three people in line to enter the room.
5. Explain that these participants are in the pose of three people playing football, but you think the statue could be improved.
6. The three newcomers have 30 seconds to make two adjustments to each of the participants' poses

to enhance them and make them look more like football players in action. They do this by directing the statues to move their body parts (e.g., raise this arm, tilt that head, put this knee on the ground).

7. When finished, have the three newcomers replace the original statues, adopting the new poses identically.

8. Invite three more people into the room and repeat Steps 5–7 until everyone has had input into the statue.

Ask these questions . . .

➤ How did you feel when I said you had to improve the statue? *(I was glad, because I couldn't even tell what they were supposed to be until you told us; I didn't want to be critical of what they had done; I couldn't think of any way to improve it.)*

➤ When you had to improve the statue, did you work together? *(No, I fixed Cary, she fixed Chris, and Chris fixed Dale; Yes, we quickly saw that all three statues needed to look more excited; No, I pretty much told the other two how to fix things.)*

➤ If we put the original three participants in their original pose next to this finished statue, how different would they look?

➤ What were some of the most original changes made? *(She moved completely to that side; At first he was catching the ball, but now he's throwing it; He turned into a referee.)*

➤ When did some changes actually mirror a pose that had been present before? *(We kept switching the way she was throwing the ball back and forth between two basic poses; He was kneeling like that near the beginning and then got up and then was back kneeling again.)*

➤ How often do we feel that having input means we

must change something, even if it's already good as is?

➤ How can we use what we learned about creativity back on the job?

Tips for success . . .

➤ For smaller groups, make the statue with just two people at a time. For larger groups, make the statue with four or more people at a time. It is best to have at least four iterations of the statue before the Debrief. The more iterations, the richer the discussion afterward.

➤ Don't give any hints or help to the participants as they improve the statue; let them figure it out for themselves.

➤ As more participants work on the statue, make sure those already in the room stay quiet. Remind them that there will be plenty of time to discuss things after everyone has had a chance. (Have them stifle their snickers as some "improvements" make the statue look like it did just a few iterations ago!)

Try these variations . . .

➤ The subject of the statue can be anything:
_ Performing an opera.
_ Doing the work that your organization does.
_ Being with a small child at the zoo.
_ Re-creating a scene from *The Wizard of Oz*.
_ Riding an amusement park ride.
_ Walking on an icy sidewalk.
_ Enjoying a day at the beach.

➤ For groups comfortable with touching, have them actually move the statues' body parts in Step 6 rather than giving directions.

For virtual teams . . .

This activity isn't suitable for virtual teams.

THE SWAMP

This is . . .   An activity in which teams are challenged with moving themselves across a room on top of flip chart paper to avoid stepping in "the swamp" (on the floor).

The purpose is . . .   For participants to learn creative problem solving as well as working together as a team.

Use this when . . .
- ➤ Individuals are not being creative in their approaches to problem solving.
- ➤ The group feels a need to compete with everyone, even within itself, rather than find ways to cooperate and collaborate.

Materials you'll need . . .
- ➤ A pad of flip chart paper.

Here's how . . .
1. Divide the group into two teams.
2. Have the teams go to opposite corners of the room.
3. Give each team half as many pieces of flip chart paper as there are members, plus one.
4. Have the teams place their papers on the floor, and all team members must stand on the paper (most will have to double up).
5. No one may touch the floor again—it is a swamp.
6. The goal is for each team to get all of its members across the room to the opposite corner (the teams

will be switching places) without any team member ever touching "the swamp."

7. Give them 10–12 minutes to accomplish the task.

For example . . .
If the team has eight members, it gets five pieces of flip chart paper (half of 8 is 4, plus 1).
If the team has four members, it gets three pieces of flip chart paper (half of 4 is 2, plus 1).
If the team has nine members, it gets five or six pieces of flip chart paper (half of 9 is 4.5, plus 1, and then round up or down).

Ask these questions . . .
➤ How did you get across the room? *(We had every one stay back while he took two sheets of paper and moved one person across at a time; We moved everyone en masse as we shifted the paper underneath us.)*
➤ Did you cooperate with the other team? Why or why not? *(No, you didn't say we had to; Yes, we realized they had a similar goal, and we could leverage all the paper better if we cooperated; No, we wanted to win.)*
➤ What about my instructions made you think this was a contest to be won? *(I guess we just assumed that; You told us what the goal was, and we figured that meant we had to do it faster than the other team.)*
➤ What kinds of assumptions are we making on the job that get in the way of truly creative solutions?
➤ How can we avoid such assumptions and be more creative?

Tips for success . . .
➤ Plain flip chart paper works better than the kind with the stickiness across the top.
➤ Don't help the teams find solutions; let them wrestle with the problem and come up with their own methods.

➤ Be sure not to call this a "race" or anything else that encourages them to think about competing with each other.

➤ Watch for the teams to compete or cooperate with each other. If you set it up properly, most will assume it's a contest when it really isn't.

➤ Watch for self-imposed limitations as well as creative solutions. For example, "Who said you couldn't rip the paper up?" One of the best solutions is to rip it into small pieces that fit under everyone's shoes. Then everyone can "skate" across the swamp quickly and easily to the other side.

Try these variations . . .

➤ Make it a competition between the two teams, explicitly.

➤ Divide the group into four teams, one in each corner. Make them cross to opposite corners. The confusion in the middle will offer great material to discuss during the Debrief.

➤ Make one or more of the team members blind-folded.

➤ Give fewer flip chart papers (half the number in the group, minus one).

For virtual teams . . .

This activity isn't suitable for virtual teams.

CHAPTER 7

Support: Activities to Appreciate and Help Each Other

ANONYMOUS FEEDBACK

This is . . . An activity in which participants offer an opinion in writing and then get anonymous feedback about it from others.

The purpose is . . . For participants to start giving honest feedback to each other anonymously. This will help prepare them to give similar feedback more directly in person.

Use this when . . .
➤ The group is more concerned about "playing nice" than being honest.
➤ The group doesn't engage in healthy debate when differences in opinions arise.
➤ Individuals hold back what they think for fear of retribution, uncomfortable conflict, or hurting others' feelings.

Materials you'll need . . .
➤ An index card for each participant.
➤ A pen or pencil for each participant.

Here's how . . .
1. On an index card, each participant writes his or her opinion about an organizational issue, decision, problem, value, or similar topic.
2. Everyone passes their card to the person to their left.
3. Participants read the cards and write a number from 1 (low) to 5 (high) depending on how strongly they agree with the statement.

4. After 30–60 seconds, have the participants pass cards again to the left.
5. Repeat the process until the cards make their way back to their authors.
6. Allow participants a moment to review the level of agreement (or disagreement) on their cards, and then discuss.

For example . . .

The topic for the index cards can be safe or explosive, depending on how ready your group is to share opinions openly. You can explore such ideas as how to solve a problem, what they think of the organization's new logo, where money can be saved from the budget, or why goals are not being met.

Ask these questions . . .

➤ What surprised you most about the numbers on your card? *(I couldn't believe how many people feel as strongly as I do about this; I was surprised at how lukewarm everyone's response was—all 3s.)*

➤ How honest were you with the numbers you gave the statements on the index cards? *(Pretty honest, because I knew the person I disagreed with wouldn't be able to confront me; I knew some people know my writing, and I was concerned they'd know whether I agreed with them or not.)*

➤ How honest were you with what you wrote on your own index card? *(Very honest, I always say what I think; I tempered it a little because I didn't want to ruffle feathers on this one.)*

➤ What keeps us from being more open and honest with each other?

➤ How can we promote more open, honest discussion together?

Tips for success . . .

➤ Encourage participants to randomly place their numbers on the cards so it's not obvious to the author who wrote what number based on the order it was written.

- ➤ Post the agreement scale for participants to reference: 1 = disagree strongly; 2 = disagree; 3 = neutral; 4 = agree; 5 = agree strongly.
- ➤ Encourage complete anonymity, even when some participants want to show off how comfortable they are at being open. While they may think they are helping, the reluctant ones will tend to retreat further if anonymity is compromised.
- ➤ Avoid making this a contest by asking things such as "Who got the most 5s?", "The least 1s?" "What were the averages?" Discourage this kind of discussion if participants start it up. It's not about the consistency of responses.

Try these variations . . .

- ➤ Use a scale of 1–4 so that no one can select a neutral position.
- ➤ This variation is for groups that are ready to take the activity a step further. After the activity, have each participant stand and read his or her card aloud. Want to go even further? Ask anyone who agreed strongly ("5") to stand and say "Yes, I agree!" Ask anyone who disagreed ("1" or "2") to stand and say "Yes, I disagree." No further discussion (or argument) is necessary. Just let the group experience disagreement *without* the conflict.
- ➤ Start with cards that already have statements written on them (you prepare in advance). Pass them around and then discuss afterward. Because no one in the group wrote the card, it will be easier to discuss.
- ➤ Merely writing something on the card may be difficult for some, because others will know who wrote a particular card. If this is a problem, you may have to shuffle the cards before people get to

read them. Have participants put a code number or symbol on the back of their card so that after the exercise you can get the right card back to its author.

For virtual teams . . . This activity works well if participants can forward e-mails without leaving their own return address on the e-mail.

1. Create and distribute a list of participants to everyone.
2. Each participant writes his or her opinion in an e-mail and sends it to the next person on the list after his or her own name.
3. Participants read the e-mail and enter a number into the e-mail from 1 (low) to 5 (high), depending on how strongly they agree with the statement.
4. Participants then forward the e-mail on to the next person on the list after their own name.
5. Repeat the process until the e-mails make their way back to their authors.
6. Allow participants a moment to review the level of agreement (or disagreement) on their e-mails, and then discuss.
7. All but the last variation listed can work for a virtual team.

 **GARBAGE**

This is . . .   An activity in which participants write down a problem they are struggling with and then get help from others on how to approach it.

The purpose is . . .   For participants to help each other think outside the box to find solutions.

Use this when . . .
- ➤ Individuals are distracted from a meeting or training by other concerns.
- ➤ Individuals need to see the value of others' help and input.
- ➤ Individuals are having trouble seeing creative solutions to difficult problems.

Materials you'll need . . .
- ➤ A piece of paper for each participant.
- ➤ A pen or pencil for each participant.
- ➤ A clean wastebasket or similar sized receptacle.

Here's how . . .
1. On a piece of paper, participants describe a problem, concern, or issue they want help with.
2. Participants then crumple up their papers and throw them into a clean wastebasket or other receptacle.
3. Ask someone to pick one crumpled paper from the wastebasket and toss it to someone else.
4. The recipient of the crumpled paper forms a problem-solving team by selecting two others with whom he or she would like to work. The team is formed before he or she reads the paper.

5. Repeat Steps 3 and 4 until everyone is in a problem-solving team.

6. Each three-person team now has 3 minutes to come up with solutions, ideas, or suggestions for what's on the paper.

7. After the 3 minutes, each team takes 1 minute to report on its issue and suggested solution.

Ask these questions . . .

➤ How many of you got one or more ideas that will truly help you with the problem you wrote on your paper? *(Show of hands.)*

➤ Why did you choose who you did for your team? *(I knew whatever the issue was, she would have good ideas; He and I rarely get to work together, so I wanted an opportunity; She knows how to help me get past my indecisiveness.)*

➤ How did you feel having to give advice on a problem that was not yours? *(Who am I to help this person; I didn't feel confident with my lack of understanding; Ready to pitch in and help as best I could.)*

➤ Why don't we ask each other for help more often? *(I don't want to impose on others; I figure they don't know my work well enough to help; I'm supposed to find solutions—that's what I'm paid to do.)*

➤ How can we encourage each other to seek help more often back on the job?

➤ What should we do about the crumpled papers we didn't get to today?

Tips for success . . .

➤ Prevent participants from being on a team to address the paper that they wrote.

➤ Encourage people to write clearly so that the papers can remain anonymous.

➤ Offer a few examples of what may be appropriate to write on the papers if participants need help getting started.

> Steer the conversations away from becoming "gripe sessions" by encouraging a focus on solutions.

> You may want to use more creative or more random ways to have the teams form.

> Encourage the problem-solving teams to force themselves to come up with ideas or suggestions, even if they don't have enough information. This isn't about solving the problem perfectly. It's about prompting creative thinking for the problem's owner(s).

> Discourage the problem owners from criticizing any help they get from the problem-solving teams. Their responses should be limited to "thank you."

Try these variations . . .

> Further drive the activity by suggesting limits on what to write on the paper (e.g., customer service issues, quality issues, teamwork issues).

> Don't solve the problems at all. Use the waste-basket as a "holding tank" for the problems and encourage participants to let the problems sit there during the meeting or training so that they can focus on the topic at hand.

> For major problems or major help, have the teams take their papers with them to work on and report back to the group at a later date.

For virtual teams . . .

This activity isn't suitable for virtual teams.

ONE WORD

This is . . .	An activity in which participants acknowledge and recognize their peers' strong points using just one word to describe them.
The purpose is . . .	For participants to receive recognition and appreciation from each other and have it reinforced by the whole team.
Use this when . . .	➤ A significant project or work effort has been completed—to celebrate the success. ➤ Individuals are feeling down or less confident about themselves. ➤ Individuals need to recognize and appreciate what's going right among themselves. ➤ Individuals need to bond together.
Materials you'll need . . .	➤ Index cards. ➤ Pen or pencil for each participant.
Here's how . . .	1. Give each participant as many index cards as there are other participants. 2. At the top of each card, the participants write the other participants' names—a different name on each card. 3. Below each name, the participant then writes ONE WORD that best describes the person whose name is on that card. 4. Have everyone share their words with the group, explaining briefly why they chose that word for that person. 5. After sharing, give participants the cards with their names on them as reminders of what was said about them.

For example . . .

"My word for Steven is CONNECTOR. He's so good at connecting people with other people. I admire the way he can just strike up conversations with just about anyone and then find a way to connect that person to someone else he knows who will benefit by the connection."

"My word for Dale is SELF-RESPECT. I love the way he's able to stick up for what he needs and what's important to him without having to be selfish or demanding or overbearing. It's clear he respects himself as much as he does others—there's a good healthy balance there."

Ask these questions . . .

➤ How difficult (or easy) was it for you to give others positive recognition? Why? *(It was easy because I do it all the time; It wasn't as bad as I expected it to be; It was hard not to start crying.)*

➤ How does this kind of recognition differ from what you receive from me and other bosses? *(This felt more real because it's from my peers; This felt forced because they had to do it; It felt genuine because they could have chosen other words, but didn't.)*

➤ What if we gave feedback like this to others outside our group (e.g., vendors, internal customers, support staff)?

Tips for success . . .

➤ Afterward, give the cards to the participants that have their names on them so they can have a record of what others said.

➤ There may be a tendency for some participants to dismiss the positive feedback they get, minimize it, or rationalize it away. You may have to make a ground rule that the only thing the recipient of feedback can say is "thank you."

➤ Make sure the explanations remain brief, or you'll quickly run out of time and some team members may be cheated out of hearing their words.

Try these	➤ If time is short, focus on only one person. Give
variations . . .	each participant one card to write a word for that
	one team member. Next meeting, focus on an-
	other team member until eventually you've cov-
	ered them all.

➤ Structure this further by announcing that the word has to be work related (avoiding things like "beautiful" or "health conscious" or "grand-mother"). You may want the word to be related to a specific project or work responsibility.

➤ Specify that participants liken the person to an animal, food, color, movie character, or some other descriptor. This will make it more difficult for some, but others will feel this allows for greater creativity. Then describe why you chose this animal, food, color, etc., for this person.

➤ Have the participants start by writing one word on each card NOT associated with anyone. Just write characteristics of good team players. Then, ask participants to take the cards and assign one to everyone in the group. Some will be natural matches. Others may have to be force fit, but still, the logic in the force fittings will be telling.

For virtual teams . . .

This activity works well regardless of the technology used.

1. Make sure each location has a set of index cards.
2. Follow the steps above.
3. For virtual teams that do not have audio, type in the word, followed by the reason.
4. Rather than hand the cards over, each participant can e-mail their word to the receiver of that word. The cards can also be sent to the receiver through regular mail.

POSITIVE ENVELOPES

This is . . . An activity in which participants give each other positive feedback in writing.

The purpose is . . . For participants to give and receive recognition and appreciation to and from each other.

Use this when . . .
- A significant project or work effort has been completed, and it's time to celebrate success.
- Individuals are feeling down or less confident about themselves and need to recognize what's going right among themselves.
- Individuals need to bond together.

Materials you'll need . . .
- One envelope for each participant.
- A pen or pencil for each participant.
- Index cards.

Here's how . . .
1. Have the group sit in a large circle.
2. Give each participant as many index cards as there are other participants.
3. Have participants write their own name in large letters on the front of their envelope.
4. Then have them pass their envelope to the person on their right.
5. Each participant thinks of something positive to say about the person whose envelope they are now

holding. They write it down and put that index card in the envelope.

6. After 1 minute, the participants again pass that envelope (with their comment card inside) to the right.

7. Repeat Steps 5 and 6 until the envelopes make their way around the group and back to the original owners.

8. Give the participants a few moments to read through their comment cards.

For example . . .

"Megan. I love how you are your own person. You are not closed to other people, but you do not let them dictate who and what you are either!"

Ask these questions . . .

➤ How difficult (or easy) was it to give each other recognition? *(It was easier writing it than saying it would have been; It was hard to put into words how I felt.)*

➤ Did the fact that it was written make it more or less difficult? *(It was easier because I didn't have to see their reaction, I could just write; It was harder to come up with just the right words because it was going to be on a paper that may be kept a while.)*

➤ How does recognition you get from your peers differ from recognition you get from me? *(It means more because they aren't paid to recognize me; It means the same, feedback is feedback; I like it because they know my work better than you do.)*

➤ What if we spoke this kind of feedback to each other more often?

Tips for success . . .

➤ Encourage participants to write the first thing that comes to mind—usually it's the most appropriate.

➤ Discourage participants from helping each other think of something to write down (the feedback should be their own, not someone else's).

Try these
variations . . .

➤ Be more specific about what the comments should reference—teamwork, leadership qualities, contribution to the project, and so forth.
➤ Have the participants try to guess who wrote which comment.
➤ Have the participants post their cards on a larger sheet of paper so that everyone can see and appreciate.
➤ With a well-established, highly performing team, have the participants offer a suggestion to the individual on how he or she could improve his or her performance.
➤ Encourage the participants to sign their names on the cards.

For virtual
teams . . .

This activity works well if participants can forward e-mails quickly.

1. Create and distribute a list of participants to all participants.
2. Each participant sends an e-mail to the next person on the list with just their own name in the body of the e-mail.
3. Follow the steps above. Instead of using cards and envelopes, add to the e-mail and forward it to the next person on the list.
4. Repeat the process until the e-mails make their way back to the person whose name is at the top of the e-mail.
5. A variation: Do this activity during the course of a week or more rather than during a specific meeting.

SECRET COACH

This is . . . An activity that encourages all participants to help each other succeed during a meeting.

The purpose is . . . For participants to practice coaching and helping each other actively participate in a meeting.

Use this when . . .
- ➤ Individuals are focusing too much on themselves.
- ➤ Individuals are not cooperating well.
- ➤ You don't have prep time and/or materials for anything more elaborate.

Materials you'll need . . .
- ➤ Slips of paper with each participant's name on a separate slip.

Here's how . . .
1. Randomly distribute name slips to each participant.
2. Make sure no one gets his or her own name.
3. Tell participants to help and encourage the person whose name they have to be successful in the meeting.
4. They are to do this without anyone being able to guess whose name they have.
5. Conduct the business meeting.
6. Afterwards, have the participants try to guess who their Secret Coach was.

For example . . . I have Doug's name but notice that neither Doug nor David have spoken up yet. I don't want others to see that I have Doug's name, so I say, "Wait a minute. I don't think we've heard from everyone. Doug, David, what do you both think about this proposal?"

Ask these questions . . .

➤ How did you know who your Secret Coach was? *(She kept looking at me; He prompted me to talk; She listened more attentively to me than she usually does.)*

➤ How did you feel when others offered you support even when they ended up not being your Secret Coach? *(It felt more like a team; Like others cared; Like we were really connecting.)*

➤ How did it feel to be a Secret Coach for someone else? *(I felt like I was helping someone; I felt a little self-conscious; Like I was pushing; I felt closer to my teammate.)*

➤ What if we continued this beyond just today's meeting?

Tips for success . . .

➤ State up front that they can't guess who their Secret Coach is until after the meeting (otherwise, people start guessing the minute anyone says anything to anyone else).

➤ Explain the strategy that in order to not be detected as someone's Secret Coach, they will have to spread their coaching around to others as well.

➤ Set the example of coaching early in the meeting to put others at ease with the behavior change you're asking for.

Try these variations . . .

➤ Have the group try to guess who had who's name rather than each individual trying to guess who had his or her name.

➤ Extend the game beyond a meeting to a whole day or even a phase of a project. Reward prizes at the end of the time period to Secret Coaches who went undetected. Be careful not to focus too much attention on secrecy or the Secret Coaches may become inactive just to avoid detection!

➤ Give each participant two people to coach. Rather than being secret about it, make the object to balance the coaching so that both team members feel equally coached.

For virtual teams . . .

This activity works well regardless of the technology used.

1. Randomly distribute the names to the Secret Coaches via e-mail or discreet instant message.
2. Follow the steps above.
3. Each of the variations listed can work for a virtual team.

TOMBSTONE

This is . . . An activity in which participants create epitaphs for a team member who is leaving the team or for a project that is ending.

The purpose is . . . Participants reflect on (and appreciate) the success of a project or qualities of a team member who is leaving.

Use this when . . .
- A team member is leaving the team.
- A project is concluding.
- A significant work period (e.g., end-of-the-year rush, budget season) has ended.

Materials you'll need . . .
- A large piece of poster board or piece of flip chart paper for each team.
- Several different colored markers for each team.

Here's how . . .
1. Divide the group into teams of 2–5 members each.
2. Give each team a poster board or piece of flip chart paper and several markers.
3. Each team creates a tombstone with an epitaph honoring a team member who will be leaving the team shortly or celebrating a project that is ending.
4. Share the tombstones with each other and then give them to the departing team member as a memento, or place a project tombstone in a common area.

For	"Here lies Keesha.
example . . .	She shared her knowledge.
	She shared her expertise.
	But she sure never shared her peanut M&Ms!"

"Beloved Project XYZ.
So much experience for all of us.
We only wish there had been more X than Y or Z!"

Ask these	➤ What was the first thing that came to your mind
questions . . .	for the epitaph? *(How much we'll miss her technical expertise; How hard we worked together on that project; That he really helped more than even he thinks he did.)*

➤ What other things did you want to say to the team member that didn't get on the epitaph? *(She needs to leave a cheat sheet for her desk; He was great at bringing humor to the group.)*

➤ What other things did you want to mention about the project that didn't get included in the epitaph? *(That we helped change the culture around here with the whole approach to inclusion; That we weren't even trying to save money but we did; That we should have recorded our processes in more detail.)*

➤ Why do you think we wait until someone is leaving before telling that person how much we appreciate him or her?

➤ How can we show greater appreciation to each other before we leave the team?

Tips for	➤ Don't help the participants. Let them use their
success . . .	creativity. Emphasize creativity and genuineness over being "right" or "correct."

➤ Separate the teams as much as possible—into different rooms if they are available. The less they overhear each other, the more original their own work will be.

Try these	➤ Replace the materials with a slab of clay and a
variations . . .	stick. Teams shape the tombstone first, and then
	carve their epitaph into its face.

➤ Replace the materials with a large styrofoam board and stick. Teams carve into the board. They can then paint or otherwise decorate it.

➤ Require that the epitaphs be in a format such as a poem.

➤ Have each person make one tombstone. Gather all the tombstones and display them as a "graveyard" for the project.

For virtual teams . . . This activity works well with teams that can see each other and in which the number of participants at each location is roughly the same.

1. Make sure each location has a set of materials.
2. Participants at each location form a team.
3. Follow the steps above.

TOTEM POLES

This is . . . An activity in which participants build a totem pole together to represent their team.

The purpose is . . . For participants to see how their individual skills and qualities will complement others' to form an integrated, unified team.

Use this when . . .
- ➤ A new team is forming or new members are joining a team.
- ➤ The group is devaluing one or more of its members.
- ➤ The group has not come together as a team yet.

Materials you'll need . . .
- ➤ One toilet paper tube for each participant.
- ➤ Craft supplies, such as markers, construction paper, scissors, tape, glue, pipe cleaners, yarn, beads, and so forth.

Here's how . . .
1. Divide the group into teams of 4–9 members.
2. Distribute the toilet paper tubes and craft supplies.
3. Give participants 6 minutes to individually create an animal with their toilet paper tube. The animal should have some meaning or symbolism to its creator.
4. Have the teams join their tube animals together to make a totem pole.
5. Each team presents its totem pole to the rest of the group, explaining the animals used and their meanings.

Ask these questions . . .	➤ How did you decide which animal to create? *(I'm pretty shy so I made a giant squid; I wanted my animal to show how impatient I get with mediocre performance; I needed to show my tenacity.)*

➤ How did you decide which animal to create? *(I'm pretty shy so I made a giant squid; I wanted my animal to show how impatient I get with mediocre performance; I needed to show my tenacity.)*

➤ How did you determine where each animal went on the totem pole? *(We wanted to show a common thread throughout; We didn't really have an order; We wanted the totem pole to be aesthetically pleasing.)*

➤ What did you learn about your teammates through this activity?

➤ How can we continue coming together as a team back on the job?

Tips for success . . .

➤ Err on the side of having too many craft supplies rather than not enough. Creativity will blossom with more possibilities.

➤ If you are dividing the group into teams, you may want to be deliberate about who goes on which team. Force some interaction that needs to happen rather than relying on chance or (worse) allowing known cliques to regroup.

Try these variations . . .

➤ Have the teams build the animals together and then assemble the totem pole together. This way, all team members get to have input on each element. They may choose to incorporate some kind of theme with all the animals on their totem pole for more unity.

➤ Distribute the supplies to the teams in a way that forces them to barter or share supplies. For example, one team gets all the scissors, one team gets all the pipe cleaners, and so forth.

➤ After the participants have created their animals, have them trade the animals with the other teams. Each team ends up with animals they did not create. Teams then build the totem pole with the animals based on what they know of the animals' creators.

For virtual teams . . .   This activity works well with teams that can see each other and in which the number of participants at each location is roughly the same.

1. Make sure each location has a set of materials.
2. Participants at each location form a team.
3. Follow the steps above.
4. A variation: After the individuals have created their animals, have them trade their animals with another team via mail. Resume the activity at the next meeting by having the teams create a totem pole with the animals they received.

TROPHIES

This is . . .	An activity in which participants create trophies for each other to recognize qualities, skills, or achievements.
The purpose is . . .	For participants to give and receive recognition and appreciation.
Use this when . . .	➤ A significant project or work effort has been completed, and it's time to celebrate success. ➤ Individuals are feeling down or less confident about themselves and need to recognize what's going among themselves. ➤ Individuals need to bond together.
Materials you'll need . . .	➤ Aluminum foil. ➤ Slips of paper with each participant's name on a separate slip.
Here's how . . .	1. Randomly distribute name slips to each participant. 2. Make sure no one gets his or her own name. 3. Make the aluminum foil accessible to everyone. 4. Give everyone 8 minutes to make a trophy out of aluminum for the person whose name they have. 5. Have each participant stand and present the trophy to its recipient.
For example . . .	"This trophy is for Lisa. It's made like this because this top part here represents how Lisa always goes way above and beyond what's expected of her without

complaining. This long part here represents the long hours she puts in without announcing it or making a big deal about it. You can always count on her to be there, quietly getting the job done!"

<table>
<tr><td>Ask these questions . . .</td><td>

➤ How many were recognized for something you were not expecting? *(Show of hands.)*

➤ How difficult was it for you to give this recognition? *(It was easier than I expected, because she really did do a great job; It was awkward at first, we just don't talk like this to each other around here.)*

➤ Why is it important for us to take time out to recognize each other like this? *(Everyone wants to hear what they are doing well; It helps us come closer together by hearing what we appreciate about each other rather than focusing on the negative all the time.)*

➤ How can we encourage each other to give recognition like this more often back on the job?
</td></tr>
<tr><td>Tips for success . . .</td><td>

➤ The trophy can be for specific skills that are used frequently or for a specific accomplishment that the person has achieved recently.

➤ Refrain from giving too many ideas about the trophies—otherwise, they become recognition from you, not the individual giving it.

➤ If someone gets stuck, ask the group to help him or her rather than you giving hints or suggestions.
</td></tr>
<tr><td>Try these variations . . .</td><td>

➤ Use different materials (e.g., feathers, pipe cleaners, straws, buttons).

➤ Have the team create more elaborate trophies together for business partners outside the group. Present them at a later time.

➤ Divide the group into small teams. Have the teams work together to create the trophies for the names they hold collectively. With more contributing to
</td></tr>
</table>

the effort, the trophy presentation will be more richly developed.

➤ Encourage acceptance speeches, much like a night at the Oscars®.

For virtual teams . . .   This activity works well with teams that can see each other.

1. Make sure each location has a set of materials.
2. Follow the steps above.
3. Mail the trophies to their recipients afterward.

INDEX

A
ABCs, 132–134
Anecdotes, personal, 43–45
Anonymous Feedback, 162–165
Appreciation building. *See* Team-
member appreciation building
Arguments
confrontations, 140–142
debrief, 25–26

B
Balloon Battle, 66–68
Bet You Didn't Know This, 32–34
Buttermilk Line, 100–102

C
Cell Phone Rings, 35–37
Childhood memories, 53–55
Chopsticks, 69–71
Coaching, 175–177
Communication skill-building,
72–74
Competition
and team-building activities, 8
team-member, problem/solution,
21–22
Competition-building activities
common goals, working toward,
88–90
communication skill-building,
72–74
energizing activities, 66–68, 75–77

high-pressure team cooperation,
78–80
implementing solution as team,
85–87
member involvement, encouraging, 91–94
out-of-control situations, 75–77
planning/strategy skills development, 66–68
setbacks, dealing with, 81–84
teamwork, learning about, 69–71
trust-building, 95–97
Complex issues, dealing with,
100–102
Confrontations, 140–142
Connections, 103–105
Cooperation-building activities,
100–129
adjusting to others, 112–114
common vision, sharing,
123–125
complex issues, dealing with,
100–102
creativity, encouraging, 115–119
details, focus on, 120–122
familiarity, dangers of, 109–111
goal-setting, 126–127
leaders and followers, importance
of, 128–130
process improvements, 103–105
win-win solutions as possibility,
106–108

Cotton Balls, 72–74
Creativity-building activities,
    132–159
    confrontations, 140–142
    creative problem-solving,
        132–134, 138–139, 157–159
    creative self-expression, 38–39
    creative thinking, 151–153,
        166–168
    encouraging creativity, 115–119
    fun and creativity, 148–150
    new solutions to old problems,
        135–137
    originality, enhancing, 154–156
    performance-results, linking,
        143–145
    threats/risks, understanding,
        146–147
Crossing the Line, 106–108

D
Debrief
    arguing, 25–26
    conducting, guidelines for, 14–15
    dominant member, 23–25
    importance of, 14
    member lack of understanding,
        26–27
    nonparticipation, 22–23
    problems/solutions, 22–27
Details, focus on, 120–122
Directions, not understanding,
    problem/solution, 19–20
Dollar Bill, 109–111

E
Energizing activities, 66–68, 75–77

F
Failure Strategies, 135–137
Familiarity, dangers of, 109–111
Feedback to others, 162–165
Fishbowl, 138–139
Fist, 140–142
Fun and creativity, 148–150

G
Garbage, 166–168
Goal-setting
    accomplishing more, 126–127
    common goals, working toward,
        88–90

H
Haiku, 38–39
Hangman, 40–42
Heads or Tails, 43–45
Higher Lower, 75–77
High-pressure team cooperation,
    78–80
House, 112–114
Human Poker, 46–49

I
I Am . . . , 50–52
Icebreaker activities, 32–64
    anecdotes, personal, 43–45
    cell phone ring, reasons for
        choosing, 35–37
    childhood memories, 53–55
    creative self-expression, 38–39
    little-known personal facts,
        sharing, 32–34, 40–42
    mingling, 46–49
    perception of others, learning,
        50–52
    perspective sharing, 56–58
    summarizing information about
        others, 59–64
Introductory activities. *See*
    Icebreaker activities

J
Job Titles, 143–145

K
Kids' Stuff, 53–55

L
Leaders and followers, importance
    of, 128–130

Leaving team, reflections on success, 178–180
License Plates, 117–119

M
Marshmallow Dodge Ball, 78–80
Materials, broken, problem/solution, 20–21
Monsters, 146–147

N
Newspaper Costumes, 148–150
Nonparticipation, problem/solution, 17–19

O
Observer role, 11
Old problems, new solutions to, 135–137
One Syllable, 120–122
One Word, 169–171
Originality, enhancing, 154–156
Out-of-control situations, 75–77

P
Pennies and Dice, 56–58
Perception of others, learning, 50–52
Performance, linking to results, 143–145
Perspective, sharing, 56–58
Planning, skills development, 66–68
Positive Envelopes, 172–174
Problem-solving, creative, 132–134, 138–139
Process improvements, 103–105
Puzzled Vision, 123–125

R
Reach for the Stars, 126–127
Recognition of team. *See* Team-member appreciation building
Reinforcement, on-the-job, 16

S
Scramble, 59–61
Secret Agenda, 151–153
Secret Coach, 175–177
Self-expression, creative, 38–39
Setbacks, dealing with, 81–84
Snake Eyes, 81–84
Statue Maker, 154–156
Stick in the Middle, 128–130
Strategy, skills development, 66–68
Swamp, The, 157–159

T
Tablecloth, 85–87
Tall Towers, 88–90
Team-building activities
    common problems/solutions, 17–27
    competition-building, 66–97
    competition in, 8
    cooperation-building activities, 100–129
    creativity-building activities, 132–159
    Debrief, 14–15
    icebreaker activities, 32–64
    introduction to activities, 10–11
    leader role, 13–14
    objectives for, 7
    on-the-job reinforcement, 16
    pairing-up, 11
    preparation for, 8–10
    team-member appreciation building, 162–186
    team size, 11
    understanding, checking for, 12
Team-member appreciation building, 162–186
    coaching, 175–177
    creative thinking, 166–168
    feedback to others, 162–165
    leaving team, reflections on success, 178–180
    team member recognition, 169–174, 184–186
    unified team, forming, 181–183

Team Scores, 91–94
Threats/risks, understanding, 146–147
Tombstone, 178–180
Totem Poles, 181–183
Trophies, 184–186
Trust-building, 95–97

U
Unified team, forming, 181–183
Unshuffle, 95–97

V
Virtual teams
  activity/technology compatibility, 8
  anonymous feedback method, 165
  audio, use of, 37
  checking for understanding, 12, 13
  communication methods, 34, 42,
    45, 64

and competitiveness, 11, 77, 84,
  87, 90, 105, 116, 119, 150, 159
debrief, 14–15, 23–26
materials, shipping to, 9, 11, 21
pairing participants, 11
progress reports from, 13
reinforcing learning, 16
room set-up, 9
time allotments for, 10, 11
trial runs, 9
Vision, common, sharing, 123–125

W
Win-win solutions as possibility,
  106–108
Word count, 62–64

X
X,Y,Z___ Letter # 27, 115–116

ABOUT THE AUTHOR

Brian Cole Miller is the founder of Working Solutions in Dublin, Ohio. A sought-after speaker and trainer, he specializes in two areas: developing stronger leaders and building more effective teams. He provides training, coaching, and consulting to busy managers and their teams nationally and internationally, including The UPS Store, Planned Parenthood, Anthem Blue Cross Blue Shield, Communications Workers of America, msn, and VISA.

If you have a quick team-building activity that you would like to share for the next volume, please contact the author at www.Working SolutionsOnline.com.